Work
After
Patriarchy

A Pastoral Perspective

Work
After
Patriarchy

A Pastoral Perspective

Patricia Budd Kepler

To order additional copies of this book, contact:

Xlibris Corporation

1-888-795-4274

www.Xlibris.com

Orders@Xlibris.com

47217

Contents

Dedicated in love and hope to my grandchildren
and their parents.

INTRODUCTION

The fog is lifting
A new day is dawning

THIS BOOK HAS been a lifetime in the making. My years with my family as daughter, sister, wife, and mother, my relationships with friends, and my professional experiences in ministry, have all helped shape my perspectives on work. My theological worldview, which began to take shape in Seminary, is still evolving. My changing faith remains a constant foundation for my life.

Central to my discussion and our conversation in this book is the effect feminism has had on my world view. When I joined the staff of the Board of Christian Education of the Presbyterian Church, as Director of Women's Program, feminism was becoming a serious movement in the United States. My position catapulted me into religious leadership in the Movement. It was then that my consciousness was raised and I became aware of the fact that women and men live in a sexist system. I worked with many amazing women and men in religious and secular circles during those years as we dared to imagine what life could be like outside of gender roles and stereotypes.

My initial gathering of material for this book began when I was Director of Ministerial Studies at Harvard Divinity School. As one of my responsibilities I studied our curriculum for the professional degree. The traditional historic disciplines of Ministry were well covered. However there were few courses preparing students to understand and address the human condition in current context. Doing theology involves an exploration of who we are as individuals, who we are in relationship, who we are in communities, and who we are in political contexts. These matters affect our relationship with and perception of God, and our approach to Scripture.

One of the issues that was clearly of importance was the place of women in society. A piece of that puzzle was the fact that more mothers were working outside of the home and more men were taking hands-on parenting seriously. This signaled a dramatic change in our understanding of how we define ourselves as women and men and how we interface with each other and the world. This gets down to large basic theological questions such as how the world is ordered, to pragmatic questions such as how our religious communities are ordered.

At Harvard Divinity School we developed a continuing education program through which employed mothers could talk about their lives and experiences in the church. We interviewed thirty working mothers in depth. We held several meetings in which we shared, reviewed, organized, and discussed their collective wisdom.

We asked forthright questions about how women were combining working for pay and family life, how their work was affecting their marriages, what dreams they had for the future, and what new needs were emerging in their lives.

We also asked what messages they were getting from the church about their role in the world as women, and what support they were getting from their congregations for their changing life styles. We hoped to gain insights that could contribute to theological education.

This book began as a book about working mothers. I discovered that I could not talk about working mothers without talking about working fathers, and gender roles. Ultimately, we cannot discuss the changing roles of women without discussing the changing roles of men. And in that context, when we talk about work in people's lives, we have to talk about all forms of work, the work that revolves around the home and community as well as the marketplace.

When I left the Divinity School and became the Minister of the Clarendon Hill Presbyterian Church, I was privileged to share directly in the lives of people in intergenerational families. Clarendon Hill became a community committed to living and worshipping beyond sexist language and systems. Members of the congregation were living out their faith in a variety of life style patterns.

I confess that I am not an objective analyst in the matters about which I write. My bookshelves are filled with books I have read about work, feminism, women's and men's life roles, societal trends, and statistics, from multiple perspectives focused on our working lives and families. My files are filled with newspaper and magazine articles about these subjects.

But in the end, I write from my own heart and mind. Being an employed wife and mother, living in the midst of women and men who share experiences similar to mine and those who have made different life choices, respecting, listening to, and learning from each one, has shaped me more than all of the academic research I have done.

My worldview has taken form from my study, from my experiences and encounters, and from my inner explorations and personal faith journey. My ideals have been radically altered in the course of my lived life. I hope that my subjectivity, rather than being a liability, enables me to have a deeper, more immediate understanding of the matters under discussion in this book.

As we explore our lives, we will challenge old ideals. I am reminded of something Rubem Alves said when he was speaking at a Triennial Meeting of Presbyterian Women in the seventies. His words have stayed with me all these years. He said, and I paraphrase: Ideals are powerful because we often build our lives around them. When someone challenges those ideals, it is as if they are challenging the foundation on which our lives are built. People will fight back.

You may find resistance in yourself, as I have found in myself, when examining the ideals that have functioned as givens in our society. We are not only talking about how we are living out our working lives, we are redefining the foundations on which they stand.

Throughout this book, I examine the ways in which human actions and consciousness are formed by role expectations, idealized images of who we "should" be as women and men and what we "should" be doing. As we delve into our actual working lives, and look to the future, we will seek to identify those guiding ethical principles that can replace the more rigid role expectations of the past.

The ancient Adam and Eve myth, in its assignment of work roles by gender after the Fall, is very useful in identifying with clarity where we have been. For help with envisioning God's Household and Order and our own, for the future, there is no mythology to guide us. We are creating tomorrow with our own stories. We need the wisdom gleaned from previous generations, the truth gained from our own living, and the energy of the Divine Spirit to chart a new course.

Clearly our work is critical to our living, affecting our sense of identity, the course of our development through all of life's stages, and our relationships in families. These things about which we think are more than personal issues, they are vital elements of our culture's future.

As we fashion our lives at a personal level, whether we like it or not, we are shaping and reshaping powerful religious and cultural assumptions. We have a responsibility to future generations to do this intentionally.

THE CHAPTERS

In the first chapter, I lay out, in broadest outlines, the particulars of my family setting and experiences along with my religious perspectives and social context. I raise what is the central question of this book:

How can women and men share in all forms of work, pursuing jobs, keeping house, raising families, and doing volunteer work?

In the second chapter, I identify the four basic forms of human work. I describe the traditional paradigm that segregated women and men's work and the myths that have upheld it. I go on to explore what a new paradigm is beginning to look like and the social revolution it is bringing about. Accompanying this revolution are deep ethical issues.

In chapters three through six I examine each form of work. I explore the ideal myths that undergirded the patriarchal division of labor between women and men, gender dualism, ask what new directions our lives and our society are taking, and discuss the creative and challenging options that are emerging. Our new directions will be based on the deep values that we hold dear and want to incorporate into our lives. When we uncover what these are, we are ready to advocate for specific social changes.

Clearly our work is critical to our living, affecting our sense of identity, the course of our development through all of life's stages, and our relationships in families. These things about which we think are more than personal issues, they are vital elements of our culture's future.

The last chapter takes a look at how work fits into all of life and how we can take a life long view of work. Seeing life as a creative process and ourselves as partners with God, we will talk about our part in the ongoing work of shaping a new creation that is more just, more compassionate, and more sustainable.

OUR CONTEXTS

I come to these issues as a Christian Minister. We will each look at these matters from our own faith or belief perspectives, our own cultural experiences, and our family legacies. When I speak in the context of my tradition, I invite you to translate it into your own, religious or secular.

I also come as a Feminist who believes that women and men have both been oppressed by gender stereotypes, role expectations, and the false gods of power and wealth that have been worshipped in our society.

Serene Jones writes in her book *Feminist Theory and Christian Theology: Cartographies of Grace,* "Over the years of my involvement in feminist political action, I have been repeatedly struck by feminism's undaunted predilection for the future. Feminism has always been sustained by the belief that things can get better."

On November 4, 2008, the United States elected its first African American President, Senator Barack Obama. He campaigned on the premise that change can come, good change that brings hope and betterment to the nation and world. Throughout his acceptance speech, the millions of people gathered chanted "Yes, we can!"

Archbishop Desmond Tutu, coming from a faith perspective, has a concept that he refers to often in his book, *The Rainbow People of God,* "God's peace involves inevitably righteousness, justice, wholeness, laughter, joy, compassion, sharing, and reconciliation."

I believe in this vision of the future.

This does not assume a future free from struggle or discord, or even from the forces of evil. It does assume a world in which we are surrounded by a great Love that passes understanding and a steady light of compassion that can shine in human kind. And I believe we are already participating in the future when we are nourished by "streams of living water," that flow from the grace of God.

I share hope in the future. It is a basic premise of this book that "Yes, we can." We can do many things through dedicated lives and God's gracious Spirit alive among us. We can tear down the walls of gender segregated work, open windows of opportunity for both women and men to become whole and live in just relationships, in a world blessed by the human resources of men and women working together.

ACKNOWLEDGMENTS

I am more than grateful to all the people whose lives have touched mine and who have contributed to this book in such significant ways. I am especially grateful to my husband and sons. They went through the promise and upheavals of feminism with me without the support of a movement behind them.

Our sons now have families of their own who enrich our lives immeasurably. I am grateful to all the members of their families and all that I have learned from them throughout these changing times.

My family and friends have put up with me and my ruminations and helped to keep me honest. I am indebted to my family of origin and my siblings and their families who have been a constant source of support and inspiration. I owe thanks to my friends, who have walked with me, sharing life's ups and downs and plateaus. They have agreed and disagreed with me without abandoning me. All have enriched my life and added more to my education than I could ever absorb.

My husband Thomas Fitch Kepler has read this manuscript and done the final copy editing.

February 2009

CHAPTER 1

MY JOURNEY AS PRELUDE

Gentle Spirit of power
Stir up the stagnant pools
In which we swim in circles
And lure us back to life.

NO BOOK IS without bias. Our perspectives and values are part of us and part of everything we do. And that is a good thing. All of us play a variety of roles in a lifetime. At the heart of those roles is our being shining through. One of our central goals, should we decide to let it be, is letting more and more of ourselves take shape as we decide exactly how we are going to live daily life throughout the course of our changing identities; child, mother, father, grandparent, student, employee, independent contractor, professor, salesperson, consumer, member of a religious community, political party, social group, whatever.

From the beginning, I want to tell you something about who I am and where I am coming from.

GROWING UP

I think my father decided on the day I was born that I would have a career. He envisioned my becoming a lawyer and following in his footsteps. Even though I was a girl in an era when few women had professions, there was no doubt in his mind that I could, should and would have a profession. Therefore there was no doubt in my mind either.

His confidence in me encouraged me to the core of my being. What neither of us ever gave any thought to was how my career would combine with marriage and a family. I think that he assumed that I would be single. I didn't think about it at all. However, the fact that my father was both a professional, and a husband and father, did not escape my attention. I was aware that mother had given up any thought of a career after she had their second child and my father was in graduate school.

Mother had an inner spiritual strength, and unshakable religious faith. She was a calming presence and a dedicated mediator whenever disagreements arose. She was also very beautiful. While I saw my personality as being more closely aligned with my father's as a child, as I matured I became aware that I was my mother's daughter as well. And, like her, I just assumed that as a woman I would have a husband and children someday.

Looking back, I can see that my mother, in her own way, encouraged me to be all that I could be. She did this in spite of the fact that she harbored some ambivalence about it. She often wondered out loud in my presence, how a man could ever love someone with as strong a will as I had.

As it turns out, our mother, thankfully, had a very strong will of her own when it came to survival. She lived to be eighty-six in spite of almost dying from pneumonia, giving birth to a still born child, having two miscarriages, beating breast cancer, having two open heart surgeries, and almost dying from anaphylactic shock. And, oh yes, two hip replacements. Through it all, she had absolute faith in God's ability to pull her through if it was His will. And she had an amazingly up-beat attitude about life.

Our father, on the other hand, died at the age of sixty-six on the verge of retirement, suddenly and without warning, as he was correcting final exams for his beloved Drexel students. He had never been in the hospital in his life.

As a young woman growing up, I didn't really pay much attention to anything but the present. I was not into analyzing my relationship with my parents or thinking about the future. I was too busy living in the moment. I was the oldest daughter of four children. I have a sister, Mary, two years younger, and a sister Theresa, fourteen years younger. We lost our brother Harold, ten years younger, to cancer a few years ago. Along with these siblings, I am blessed by in-laws and nieces and nephews.

My siblings were very much part of my life. My sister Mary and I grew up together in the city. By the time my sister Theresa and brother, Harold, were growing up, we had moved to the suburbs. They were like a second, special family to all of us in what I think of as my parents' second adult life phase.

Although not very reflective when I was young, I was aware of how closely I identified with my father. Often this contributed to our wills tangling and creatively engaging. This closeness also enabled me to learn from him, and find my own independence. I trusted him to be there for me. I could both lean on him and stand up to him.

Father was a gifted and dynamic professor, the Director of Athletics at Drexel for several years, a busy lawyer, a trustee in our church and a dedicated teacher of an adult class. He was a good and loving provider for our family. Clearly, I admired him. I also knew his soft spots. He was generous to a fault, over-protective and very strong-minded, and incapable of holding a grudge.

I admired my mother in a different way. She was the one who held us close to our faith and the church. She had grown up as a Catholic and a devotion to church attendance that was unwavering was built into her soul. She was community minded but only accepted volunteer work that did not require any writing. As an immigrant she had never learned to write fluently in English though she spoke without an accent.

She was devoted to my father and committed to her mother who lived with us. She was more quiet than my father but brave and head-strong in her own way. She became pregnant with our younger brother, Harold, and sister, Theresa, in spite of her doctor's warning that because of her heart condition she would be risking her life if she gave birth again.

But, she survived giving birth to our brother and sister and she thrived as they gave her and my father a new lease on life. And our younger siblings gave my sister and me new life-long companions and kept us in touch with a new generation.

Growing up, I was hardly aware that mother had, as a young woman, immigrated from another country. I did not understand until I was in my twenties what courage it had taken for her to come from Germany alone by ship when she was turning seventeen. She arrived in America knowing no English, sponsored by a distant cousin. Desperately lonely, she finally found work as a governess. She loved the people she lived with and cared devotedly for their son. She met my father when she was studying English at Millersville State College.

My maternal grandmother became part of our family when she immigrated from Germany a few years later. It was after World War I and Germany was in the grip of a desperate depression. Her husband died just before they were scheduled to make the trip together. Deddy, as we called her, was warm and nurturing with me and my three siblings. She inspired me with her faith and fortitude, her friendship and great cooking.

I remember her attending Mass in the Catholic Church around the corner every morning and on Sundays. The rest of us attended the Presbyterian Church. My relationship with her was one of uncomplicated love. She was a friend and advocate on whom I relied and from whom I derived great comfort. Three special things I shared with her and my sister Mary were going to the movies together on

Saturdays (and often seeing the movie twice at my urging), lighting candles in church, and wonderful German food. I still love movies and candles and food.

Looking back, I wonder what it was like for her, leaving her home and her work as the manager of an inn to live with us and settle down to a somewhat isolated domestic life. She never fully learned to speak English. I think love made it all work out for her, and remembrance of the terrible state of depression in Germany, fear for Germany's future, and deep dislike and distrust of the young politician who was making his way into power, Adolf Hitler.

Our family was surrounded by my father's brothers and sisters and cousins with whom we formed a close and joyful bond. His father's family had immigrated from Ireland and his mother's family from Germany. We spent early childhood summers with them in a small coal mining town, Williamstown, Pa. My cousins Rosemary and Betty lived with us while attending college. Rosemary went on to become a Roman Catholic Sister.

Various relatives would drop in to see us and often attend some Philadelphia sporting event, usually baseball. The road between Williamstown and Philadelphia was well travelled. Recently, my brother and I bought second homes in Williamstown. I have often joked with my husband that we are the only people we know who have summer homes in a small, economically challenged town.

I went to grammar school in our West Philadelphia neighborhood with my sister Mary, and continued high school at Girls' High, a magnet public school in downtown center city. Being in an all-girls school meant that we girls didn't have to look to boys for leadership and sports. I got experience in school government, sports, debating, drama, and the peace club along with a solid academic education.

My sister Mary and I were very active in our church group which provided a very special peer community that supplemented our close neighborhood ties. We loved the congregation at St. Paul Presbyterian Church. My years there provided a solid foundation for my religious formation. It was there through Westminster Fellowship that my leadership skills were honed, my love of the church was nurtured, and my appreciation for church connection was developed.

When it came time to go to college, I went to Drexel Institute of Technology, now Drexel University. I had won a Latin scholarship to Wellesley with free tuition, but my father wanted me to go where room and board was free. (I lived at home.) Tuition was also free because he was on the faculty.

There is no doubt that my father and his friends kept an eye on me at Drexel, but he never interfered with my choices, academic or extra-curricular. In subsequent years, my other three siblings graduated from Drexel too. I marvel that we each managed to have our own lives, be so involved with life at Drexel, while living at home during those college years.

At Drexel University I majored in basic science my first semester thinking that I wanted to be a doctor. My background in science was weak and it only took one term for me to figure out that I was not cut out for medicine as a career. I ended up majoring in business administration with no specific vocational goal in mind. But I felt quite at home in the program while exploring my real passions in drama, sports, and religion.

MARRIAGE, PARENTING, AND MINISTRY

In my senior year of college, my parents assumed that I would go to graduate school and it seems that I did too. Medicine had been ruled out. Law was an option but I really didn't want to go into the legal partnership my father had established over the years and there was no particular kind of practice that appealed to me. The possibility of going to Seminary came into focus. When I decided to go to Seminary it seemed quite natural and right. After all, I had been deeply involved in my church youth group and in the Christian fellowship at Drexel. I loved those experiences and had found myself and my leadership potential through them.

My family was pleased with my decision. I discovered that my father had been a country preacher before he embarked on his legal career. He seemed quite at peace with and pleased about my decision to enter the ministry. My mother, a woman of deep faith, had no idea what I was going to do with my Seminary education, but she too was supportive of my decision.

When I put the pieces of my life together, theology as a career made perfect sense even though women could not be ordained when I first entered Princeton Theological Seminary. I didn't care or think about that fact, strange as it seems to me now. I was following my heart. And by the grace of God and members of my church and family, I was fully and deeply supported.

When I applied to Princeton Seminary for their ministerial program, I was rejected. My father wanted to know why and was told that that information was not available. He refused to take No for an answer and was quite persuasive in getting me an interview, probably in the interest of shutting him up.

On the big interview day, my mother drove up to Princeton with me. As I found out, I had been rejected because of my background in business rather than liberal arts. And my grades were not stellar. Acting Dean Gardner offered me a place in the Master of Religious Education program, geared primarily to women. When I naively and matter-of-factly told the Dean that the only program I was interested in was the Bachelor of Divinity, (now Master of Divinity) degree, he graciously and miraculously decided to give me a chance. I was accepted on probation. That was a fortuitous day that shaped the rest of my life!

I did just fine in Seminary and knew right away that that was where I belonged. I fell in love with theology. Then, during my second semester, I fell in love in quite another way. I fell in love with Thomas Fitch Kepler and we married in our senior year. He was the son of China missionaries; in fact China missionaries went back several generations on both his mother's and father's sides. His family had all been stateside since 1949 when the advance of the communist revolution forced them to leave China.

When we graduated, I was six months pregnant. Tom and I automatically assumed that he would be the one to look for a job. I had, however, completed and passed my ordination exams for Ministry and was one of two women, the other being Margaret Howland, to be the first to be Licensed for Ministry by Philadelphia Presbytery. When they asked me what I would do if I ever became pregnant, I said I would deal with it. In fact, I was already dealing with it and had no idea about how I was going to exercise my official status while being a mother. I simply knew that I was taking the right step.

In the year that followed, my will and heart were focused on being a good minister's wife and mother. I gave birth to our first son, Thomas Budd, in Philadelphia under the expert care of Dr. Margaret Densmore, a woman gynecologist who flew airplanes in her spare time. Throughout my pregnancy, we had gone through many transitions, a final semester of classes, my directing a play for the Seminary, our serving as Seminary Field Education students at St. Paul, graduation, and a job search.

We settled in Englishtown, New Jersey, where Tom became pastor of the First Presbyterian Church a month before Thomas Budd was born. Thirteen months later we had a second son, James Blain, and then two years later, our third son, John Harold came into the world.

I reveled in being a mother. I simply loved it. And I can honestly say I tried my best to be an ideal church spouse. That didn't work. No matter how low a profile I kept, I was nonetheless seen as a threat by one key lay woman in Tom's church. She had her hand in everything. She attacked me around utterly petty issues. Things finally came to a head when one summer during Bible School she accused me of stealing chalk from her classroom to use in mine. It was such a small thing, but it opened my eyes. I did the only thing I felt I could do: I withdrew from all activities in the church apart from Sunday worship for the sake of my husband's ministry.

Then one day I was asked to preach in a small rural church that was near by. I said a conditional, "Yes." Tom was moderating the

Session and had suggested my name. Their invitation to me was as conditional as my acceptance. The truth was, they couldn't find anyone else. Westminster Presbyterian Church was a small black congregation. In the past, they had had African Americans for ministers, but none seemed available now.

I was more ready for work of my own than I realized. I got along well with the two men who were in the congregation on the first day I preached and with others who were still involved. This turn of circumstance led me to accept a part-time call to that church in Manalapan Township in central rural New Jersey. I was pregnant with our third child, John Harold.

While Tom and I both knew I really wanted and needed to work outside of, as well as inside our home for the sake of my sanity, and peace in his church, we explained my working as a matter of economic necessity rather than as a matter of choice. We did need the money (limited as it was). I realized then that a financial rationale for my becoming a working mother was more acceptable to others and to myself than the whole truth, which was that I enjoyed being employed.

Suddenly our life style shifted. I was a working mother, albeit part-time. I was out of tune with most of the young mothers in my husband's congregation. They had time together for morning coffee and afternoon outings to the park and volunteer work in the church. I was in tune with most of the mothers at Westminster who were also working outside of the home.

Some people in Tom's church disapproved of my employment. They felt I was short-changing Tom by not living up to their image of an attentive wife. Some people made it quite clear that they felt sorry for him, being married to a woman following her own career. Then there were those who liked having the minister to themselves and didn't mind my not being on the scene at all.

There were also those members in the Englishtown Church who valued the work at Manalapan and saw an opportunity to facilitate connections between our two churches, fostering racial cooperation in a time of the emerging Civil Rights Movement and some serious community tensions.

In the course of my work at Manalapan, the Rev. Robert Beaman became an Associate Minister and his wife Jo Anne, whose father was the minister of Old Tennent, a nearby church, became a member of the congregation and a lifelong friend. Another member, the Rev. Elenora Giddings Ivory, is now Director of the World Council of Churches Public Witness Program.

All the while that this was going on in our churches, Tom and I got strong messages from some family members on both sides that my "doing my own thing" could, probably would, reflect poorly on Tom, place unfair demands on him that would interfere with his career, and threaten our marriage.

Since we had few models on whom to rely, the going was sometimes tough. But, being who we were, there was no turning back.

The truth is that cultural influences, our natures and our families' expectations were all in conflict inside us. We certainly did not know that in just twenty years many more families would be doing just what we were doing and what most of the African American families at Manalapan were already doing.

Tom and I were the first "clergy couple" in the Presbyterian Church. "Presbyterian Life" magazine did an article on us and the author wanted our assurance that we would not get a divorce before it was published!

We were, of course, by no means the first couple to be employed parents. There had been other couples before us with two careers, two jobs, and many more would follow.

As I take time to think about it, my aunt and paternal grandmother had been working single mothers after their husbands died at an early age and my maternal grandmother was a working parent too. They had been role models for me without my realizing it.

When our third son was two, I was finally ordained as a Minister of Word and Sacrament in the Presbyterian Church by Monmouth

Presbytery in New Jersey. Up until that time, though I was Licensed to preach, and had passed all of my qualifying exams for Ministry, I could not see my way clear to full ordination. Ordination meant full commissioning as a clergy person with all of its responsibilities and privileges. I saw it as a lifetime commitment and could not reconcile making that with my role as a mother of three children.

The urging of a dear family friend, and colleague in ministry, Bill Hervey, changed my mind. Bill said in essence that at that time in history the church needed me to be a full fledged Minister with voting rights in Presbytery. That would enable me to be their advocate in the days to come. He advised me to take one step at a time since I couldn't see into the future. He was active in Civil Rights and knew that an African American congregation needed a strong voice in Presbyterian and civic halls of power.

What Bill said made sense. Thus began my transformation, my owning my profession and being at home with being a working mother. I had come to realize that no one can really see into the future. Now is what we have, *carpe diem.*

In 1966, I earned a Master of Theology degree in Psychology and Religion from Princeton Seminary. Tom had earned his in Theology in 1962.

We were fortunate to have sons who were cooperative and flexible and self-motivating, jobs that enabled us to share active parenting in their early years, my extended family to pitch in during emergencies, and capable baby sitters.

We all emerge out of childhood into adulthood with some blind spots and a need to develop ever deeper insights into our own psyches. We become self aware over time. Tom and I each had our own strengths and weaknesses, and were not really prepared for the challenges of intimacy and the vagaries of life.

Tom and I had in many ways lived beyond traditional gender myths and been able to rise above them. Intellectually we knew that both men and women are fit to parent and work for pay, to do housework and volunteer work. The remnant of the myths still lived in our heads and in the society around us. Walking the walk was not always easy.

We live in the midst of history, which like a mighty ocean draws all of us into its tides and currents in one way or another. I have experienced what an impact cultural influences, mythic ideals, and stereotypes can have on our lives. My true self was able to emerge only after I tried to put these influences in their place. But even now they keep showing up.

Looking back on my life thus far, one of the greatest lessons learned was that idealized stereotypes were not sacred and did not fit everyone. Sometimes those stereotypes are blatant and obvious and at other times subtle and seductive. Our true natures and that which is holy lie quite beyond them. Images can be, after all, illusions.

I believe there are spiritual influences at work in history and in our own lives, challenging and changing us, moving us toward wholeness and more abundant life. In the Christian Church, we call this movement toward "God's Realm," – traditionally known as "God's Kingdom." This movement is not uniquely Christian. Every faith tradition at its deepest moves toward the betterment of society, toward peace and justice.

I did not always make conscious choices about how to live my life or have the intellectual or emotional tools I needed to be truly reflective. These are garnered over time. I still find myself in search of the insight and wisdom that come from awareness as I approach new life stages and experiences.

I have no choice but to live a more examined life. This is both a blessing and a nuisance. Raised awareness, and living on the other side of innocence, has its drawbacks. Naiveté is often comforting and an excuse for some serious bumbling.

Throughout my life, I have been fortunate to be loved and encouraged in my becoming. I stumbled into many of my life's directions by the gift of God's Spirit, many helping human hands, and the accident of being born in a time of historic opportunity. I chanced my way into God's new creation, by grace and some hard work and the forbearance of many. I am eternally grateful!

I admit that I did not always succeed at combining marriage with a career. Nor did Tom. There were some very difficult times in our lives and our marriage and a period during which my husband and I were officially separated and had to sort out our lives. We went through a period of rediscovering ourselves and exploring new friendships. Meanwhile our sons were navigating the challenges of their teen years in the midst of the culture of the seventies. None of us was traveling a road much traveled.

Sometimes I wish we could relive those years and follow a less dramatic path. But we cannot turn back time and I treasure some of the experiences I had during those years even as I shudder at others.

Tom and I came back together again because family, especially our sons, were so important to us. And we worked hard to make a go of it. I am grateful that we are now enjoying our grandchildren together

However, I make no judgment about those who have navigated strains in their marriage differently. Sometimes divorce is the right answer for everyone involved. No two relationships are alike and we all make decisions based on our personal circumstances and the wisdom or necessity with which we are faced. We close and open doors as we are able.

I am unable to figure out how much of our marital difficulty was due to our breaking out of old expectations that we carried in our heads and society laid on us, and how much was due to differences in our personalities and family backgrounds. It is impossible to sort out. I do know that combining parenting and employment was the only choice I could make, being me. And I am eternally grateful to have had the opportunity to do both simultaneously.

An old unanswered question of my childhood that I didn't even know enough to ask, How can doing paid work and being married and a parent fit together? now has a partial answer. You just do it. But a new question emerges, What can we do to make it easier for those who choose or need to follow this path? While this is not a "how to" book, this question is an important one for individuals and society. We can address it from many different angles.

I have come to realize that in addition to being pragmatic and secular questions, about women's and men's working lives, these are religious questions. They get to the heart of how we define humanity, how we see men and women relating to one another, how we understand the ethics of justice and love, and how we understand Divine Reality.

I ask these questions at this moment in time when raising them seems particularly crucial. I see new generations struggling with them without a vision of the context of changing paradigms. More than half of the adults in America are combining all forms of work in their daily lives, and it is still not easy to make it all fit together.

Sometimes it seems harder to combine working roles now than when I was first engaged in employment and parenting. Employee hours are longer for many when they need to be getting shorter. Lower and middle class jobs seem less secure while CEO's are making exorbitant amounts of money. There are more economic demands being made on family incomes. And there are no clear social supports for employed parents.

Today most Americans are living outside of norms that were taken for granted in my family and in the majority of families just two generations ago. We need to ask what worldviews are replacing the old patriarchal worldview that defined the work men and women were meant to do in simplistic ways. My shift in worldview came about as social patterns were beginning to change for all of us over the years.

EMPLOYMENT AND VENTURING INTO FEMINISM

I grew up in an age when the second wave of the feminist movement was in full swing and I derived great support from my sisters and brothers in both the church and secular society who believed in equality between the sexes as I moved along in my career.

I was the mother of three sons when I became a conscious feminist. I was able to observe how deeply gender stereotypes and expectations affect men as well as women. And I saw the pain in boys and men who felt that they were being blamed personally for discrimination against women when sexist systems were the real problem.

I believed and continue to believe that both men and women are conditioned and diminished by our patriarchal culture. At a simple justice level, discrimination against women needs to be addressed directly. But then, as we move to deeper levels we discover the multiple ways in which men as well as women need liberating. Culture itself is in desperate need of change. Whatever values Patriarchy once served in society have played themselves out.

My attitude toward life was deeply affected by becoming a parent. Suddenly life seemed more precious and at the same time more vulnerable. I was in awe of parenting work and the wonder and joy of bringing a new life into the world. I took my responsibility as a mother very seriously. My own life now seemed more important because a child and then children were depending on me and my husband. My husband and I were adults. Even though we needed one another, we could, if we had to, fend for ourselves. It was different.

My worldview and the societal worldview of many others began to change dramatically with the Civil Rights Movement and the struggle for racial equality. Addressing racism taught us to see how hidden structures of discrimination are built into the social organization of society, including the stereotypes constructed around the presumed differences between black and white.

Being Pastor of an African American congregation gave me the opportunity to listen to parishioner's truths about their lives. I saw first hand the obstacles they were facing and witnessed the courage and strength with which they were able to affirm life nonetheless and hold fast to faith. It was in that context that I began the long process of finding my own voice.

Following my experiences at Manalapan, I became active in the Women's Movement by being in the right place at the right time. I accepted the position of Director of Women's Program in the Board of Christian Education of the Presbyterian Church to be staff for United Presbyterian Women. I had no idea when I took that job where it would lead. A fledgling women's movement had emerged in the Presbyterian Church and was reporting to the General Assembly of our church in 1969, the first year I was in place. As a result of their work, a Task Force on Women was formed and I was assigned to be the Staff person responsible for working with them. For a year, I did this work along with my work as staff for United Presbyterian Women. Then I served as staff for women's issues full time.

The first year the Task Force on Women reported to the General Assembly of our national church our concerns were greeted with titters that turned to a wave of laughter that filled the hall populated by primarily male commissioners. I felt as if I was in Junior High again and someone had told an embarrassing joke. The thought of discrimination against women was evidently both ludicrous and threatening to many commissioners that day. How could the issue of women's role in church and society be of serious ethical concern when other more life-challenging issues were before the church? By the following year, the corporate body had stopped laughing.

In our second year, the Rev. Dr. Beatriz Melano Couch, a pioneer in Latin American Liberation Theology, gave an introduction to our report. We were friends from our Princeton days. The General Assembly of our Church responded well to Bea and had to recognize that feminist issues transcend ethnic and national boundaries.

In my position with the Board of Christian Education I traveled at least once a month. My first trip away from my family was hard. I was a traveling working mother for the first time, anxious about flying because I had three sons to come home to. In those days before cell phones, postcards and landlines kept us in touch.

I was being educated about women's situation in society along with the church. I had not given any conscious thought to the issue of societal sexism until I became an advocate for women within our denomination. I am not sure that I even processed the fact that by being an employed mother I was swimming against the tide. I was not conceptualizing gender issues.

An important part of my ongoing education was the reading of Simone de Beauvoir's *The Second Sex*. I was at first infuriated by her emphasis on women's economic independence as essential to women's liberation and empowerment. Her view of the world seemed so cold and crass, and in such contradiction to my Christian view of the world which seemed at the time to be so humane, caring and yes, comforting. Her perspective seemed so materialistic and direct. Her analysis haunted me and got through to me. She wrote:

> "Woman exhausts her courage dissipating mirages and she stops in terror at the threshold of reality." And again, "As long as she (woman) has to struggle to become a human being, she cannot become a creator."

Many women in my generation were breaking through the threshold of reality, dismantling employment barriers, entering fields once reserved for men, becoming active in the political arena, affirming their right to control what happens to their bodies, striving toward equal partnerships in heterosexual marriage and affirming the rights of same sex partners in intimate relationships. Interdenominationally, mainline churches were not only supportive, they were active advocates.

Many men in the Presbyterian Church were supporting the women who were challenging sexism, and those men were taking on new roles themselves as active parents and equal partners in marriage. We were all also continuing our involvement in Civil Rights and the Anti-War Movement while listening for voices in international Liberation Movements.

Most of us working on these issues had grown up with romanticized images of the family and fixed concepts of the proper life roles for women and men. We loved and believed in those values even when our lives veered from them. Change for us meant confronting the very ideals that had held our lives together. That was frightening. We were becoming creators of our social milieu with thousands of others as we confronted the sexism behind the very ideals that we held sacred.

In the process of challenging the ideals we had grown up with, ideals that provided the foundation not only for social institutions but for religious institutions as well, we were searching to find and define a new reality. Some women were fortunate enough to find new fulfillment in their lives. Other women lost marriages, were blocked in their career paths, or found their health deteriorating. I personally knew women who paid a high price for taking a stand as feminists in the early days of the movement. They are our unsung heroes. They were shut out of jobs for which they were qualified in the academic and religious world. They lost significant relationships. They suffered financially. They were dismissed for their perspective and worldview.

Anyone old enough to remember will recall how feminists were often maligned in the press. We were accused of hating men, of rejecting our own womanhood, of abandoning our children, of burning our bras. None of this was true for the women I knew, who affirmed their womanhood, loved men as husbands, brothers, fathers, uncles, colleagues, and friends, took good care of their children, opened new doors for future generations, and as far as I know, wore bras.

Being in the Women's Movement did not, of course, make us saints. We made mistakes. But we were on the right track in our belief in the equality of the sexes and the importance of shared roles in the family.

Some people took the position that, were it not for a few disgruntled and embittered radical women, it would be clear that life between women and men was just the way God intended – and women and men liked it that way! But many more women and men than were directly involved in the Movement knew that things had to change.

Betty Friedan's *The Feminine Mystique* had helped put the romantic notions of women's lives in ideal families in perspective. She wrote about the ways in which the home could be a trap and marriage be less than sweetness and light in its bosom. Women were dissatisfied.

Friedan helped open our eyes to the fact that women's power and influence in the world was negligible. Women's power to work behind the scenes to influence men was not enough. Women were maintaining homes, raising children, and having almost nothing to say about the world into which their children were growing, and in which they lived.

And, surprise of surprises, men did not love and respect women all the more because of the sacrifices they made on behalf of their families.

Women's groups both religious and secular pointed out that women who were employed were being paid 59% of what men were making in the same jobs, and many women were stuck in the "pink collar work ghetto." We noted that most jobs that involved the exercise of power were not in women's hands. There were few women in Congress, which amounted to a form of taxation without representation. Women and men who were employed while raising families, either as couples or single parents, faced an uphill battle because they had no social support. Most people in poverty were women and children.

Matters of simple justice were at stake as we engaged in the struggle for an Equal Rights Amendment which eventually lost by negative votes in three southern states.

Some of those critiquing feminism pitted women's sexuality and women's equality against each other.

Marabel Morgan wrote a popular book entitled *The Total Woman*, in which she describes her version of ideal womanhood. Women would submit to men as the head of the house. She discusses love in this context and then offers instructions on how to have a fun and exciting sexual life with their spouses. We subtitled her book, "The Totaled Woman."

Feminists as I knew them didn't have any trouble with putting sizzle back into sex. We just didn't like the high price women were supposed to pay for it, or the other parts of their personalities they were supposed to suppress in order to please men. Feminism challenged society's double standard when it came to sexuality

Much was achieved during Feminism's heyday. To name a few: women's enrollment in professional schools rose, mothers joined the workforce in record numbers, women began to enter fields previously reserved for men, and men entered fields once populated only by women.

Women in traditional female jobs began to organize in labor unions and to demand new professional respect. Equal Employment Enforcement codes were written to include gender and the problem of sexual harassment in the workplace gained public attention. Roman Catholic Sisters went through a radical revolution within their orders: changing from habits to street clothes and living in the communities within which they worked if they so chose. More fathers became active parents, becoming comfortable being seen in public caring for their children. And more families held off poverty by the efforts of two employed parents.

Over time, the deeper ideological issues beneath the movement began to emerge. In the theological realm, we challenged male dominance over women in positions of power, and exclusive use of male pronouns for God. We developed worship material that used inclusive language for humanity and God. We challenged the ways in which religious communities had defined women and men and objected to the gender divide that this fostered. Heterosexual marriage was seen as being in need of reform and discrimination against homosexuals was identified as a matter of social justice that needed to be addressed.

I witnessed the journey of liberal men and women in the church who stood for justice, integration, an end to poverty, and peace. We had been advocates for an end to segregation. We had fought hard for ending the Vietnam War. We called for all manner of change in the social fabric of our nation which tolerated these injustices and were defenders of civil liberties. We became active in the war on poverty and in liberation theology. And when the Women's Movement emerged, many women and men stood together in defense of women's rights. The effects of sexism on men's lives were never examined by the general public though men and women in the Movement had begun to address them.

The women's liberation movement was different from all the others in that it came close to home. This movement challenged deeply-held religious ideals about women's and men's nature and relationships, and rightful places in life in both the home and society. Every other movement was about rights in the wider social milieu. This movement spilled over into the privacy of our homes and into our intimate relationships.

The Movement years had also been years of experimentation with drugs, communal living, and more sexual freedom. Some people came to equate feminism with these social issues. They began to call for a return to the "good old days and ways" while others continued to believe that feminism held promise for the betterment of everyone's lives.

When I became Director of Ministerial Studies at Harvard Divinity School, I was no longer advocating for gender equality as a job. I was now in a position to implement the things we had worked for in this new ecumenical, academic setting. In hiring personnel for our programs, designing courses, teaching, and working with other faculty, I found that feminism had permeated my soul. I was past the consciousness-raising stage, I was now about living my beliefs. I was in a new job in a new city with three teen-age boys. Being an employed mother took on new meaning.

I took the position at Harvard and moved to Boston with our sons when Tom and I were separated. Parenting as a single mother was a real challenge. My older son patiently explained to me why this was. He said that women were not known for having authority. In school, the only women they had ever heard of who had authority were queens – like the Queen of England – and everyone knew they relied on male advisors for their decisions.

Whether or not women were supposed to have authority as a class, I, as Director of the professional degree program at Harvard and as a parent was definitely supposed to have some! I pursued work in both arenas with enthusiasm. While I was at Harvard, Tom and I got back together again and parenting became much easier.

In addition to my work at the Divinity School, I was doing volunteer work as President of the Women's Coalition for the Third Century, a Bicentennial organization. While I was at Harvard, we finalized our "Declaration of Interdependence" and "Declaration of Imperatives." Those documents signaled the fact that while we still stood by the importance of women's rights, we believed that women as well as men had a responsibility to fashion the future of society.

In a Coalition celebration of the Bicentennial, we produced a musical entitled "Eve and Adam and the Curse." Thomas Budd Kepler and Douglas Ruffle wrote the score and I wrote the lyrics and directed it. It was the beginning of my playful contending with that myth about creation.

Following my five year term at Harvard Divinity School, I became Pastor of Clarendon Hill Presbyterian Church. Tom and I had worked there as part-time Co-Pastors. When the church decided that in order to survive, it needed a pastor full-time, Tom could not apply as he already had a full time job outside of the church. I applied for the work and was chosen. Thus I began what was to be a seventeen year ministry in which, among other things, we began to implement in practice the theories our national church had propounded around issues of gender equality. We also studied sexuality and the church and became advocates for gay rights.

We never moved away from our feminist agenda as we added new areas of interest to our religious life. Increasingly the church became involved in international issues. Palestinian and Lebanese families in our midst introduced us to issues in the Middle East. African families introduced us to the Cameroon and Kenya. And we addressed these relationships in the context of our faith and deepening spirituality.

During the Clarendon Hill years, our sons were maturing and were facing decisions about education and their life-work. Parenting took on new dimensions. Financially, the options were limited by our economic situation. We were not poor enough for significant college aid and not wealthy enough to pay private school tuition. Eventually, two of our sons went to UMass Boston and our third son, after a year of college, discovered that he was a gifted carpenter and contractor and went into that field. They all married and began families.

When I retired from the church, I accepted the position of Interim University Chaplain at Tufts University. In that position my commitment to Interfaith dialogue deepened as I worked with Jewish, Muslim, Catholic, and Protestant Chaplains and emerging groups of Buddhists and Baha'is on Campus.

My work with students who were going to make decisions about their work in the years ahead, and my work in the interfaith arena, rekindled my interest in gender issues in an immediate and more complex way. These students would have to decide how to combine their evolving personal family life with their chosen careers, just as I had. My own family responsibilities now shifted to grandparenting and enjoying our grown sons and their spouses.

Meanwhile, the religious pendulum was swinging. Liberals were out, conservatives were in. Mainline denominations were close to the edge and mega churches were on the rise. While all of this was going on, religion became a less significant force in American life, at least in urban areas. Religion was out and spirituality was in. As our nation turned toward conservatism, the right became the holder and protector of family values. While those values were not explicitly identified as patriarchal, that is what they were.

Through the Movement days we had perhaps not emphasized our commitment to family values enough. We sought the realignment and redefining of power and wealth. We were trying to understand the things that make for peace. We deplored violence. We didn't have all the answers, but we were asking the right questions in these arenas. Changes in our ways of being in the world were already in motion.

CHANGE AND MORE CHANGE

In the West and in elite sectors of other countries, we had entered the electronic age with a vengeance. Information technology was at our finger tips, iPod and MP3 music in our ears, cell phones in our pockets, digital TV in our homes, internet connecting us across the world. We have new entertainment, games to play, YouTube and Facebook to explore, and explicit sex at the click of a mouse.

The world was in our homes and neighborhoods. Mega Corporations operated beyond national boundaries. We became an internationally connected world with little international governance. In the United States that meant outsourcing many jobs and importing many products, especially from China.

In terms of social movements, we had not yet learned to harness the electronic age and connect it to community organization and well being until the Presidential Campaign of 2008. When the campaign began, it had been more than thirty years since the Women's Movement and other Liberation Movements had been in their heyday.

Nationally, we had experienced years of conservative support for the wealthy and the build-up on national debt. We were involved in military action with Iraq and Afghanistan. Military might had been touted as a path to peace. We had fallen into a period in time during which ends seem to justify any means, human rights had been compromised in the name of security, and democracy. On the home-front, credit card usury had become acceptable practice as had questionable mortgage practices. Economic collapse was on the horizon.

Then came the promise of political change.

Senator Hillary Clinton, a woman, was a serious candidate for the Presidency in her bid for office in 2008 running against Senator Barack Obama. They were not the first minority candidates to run: an African American woman, Shirley Chisholm, had been a candidate for the Democratic nomination for President in 1972. Geraldine Ferraro had been the Vice-Presidential nominee with Walter Mondale in 1984. In the 2008 election, Senator John McCain, running on the Republican ticket, chose Sarah Palin as his running mate.

In the year leading up to the 2008 election, society had seemed to grow more and more schizophrenic over the issues of women's and men's appropriate roles in life, and the nature of the family. People gave lip service to women's equality but were not sure where to go with the issue after that. What about the men? The social progress brought about by human rights and antiwar movements had, for a time, been put on hold. Now it was coming back and undergoing a metamorphosis.

Barack Obama won the election as a people's candidate. His opponent in the Democratic primary, Hillary Clinton, became Secretary of State. Change is in the air and perhaps we are entering a time of black and white together and women and men together. Racism and sexism are still with us. The dream is that those who want to eradicate these systems can address them together.

As I complete this book, Tom and I have served briefly as interim pastors at a Church where the congregation is blending members from European and African descent. And we are serving another interim ministry at another church with their part-time co-pastor. There among the congregants are people of differing sexual orientations and ethnic backgrounds, and people with physical and mental challenges. These congregations remind me of what a diverse and complex society we are in America, and how blessed our churches can be when we minister in the midst of this reality.

It is in our new political and social context and my new religious adventures that I write about work roles and patriarchy in our time. As I do, I look back on where we have been, in order to go forward. We travel on new terrain as individuals, as families, and as a society in continuity with all that has gone before.

The relationships between women and men in the context of the diverse families we create, provide a foundation on which to build the whole of society. Identifying the values we cherish in those connections is part of the unfinished revolution begun in the movements of the sixties and seventies. Examining those values in light of our theological understandings can bring us a breath of fresh air.

I write about work in the midst of our changing economic as well as social environment. Americans are facing real financial issues: soaring housing prices and taxes, the collapse of the housing market, rising credit card debt, rising gas prices, and the remnants of a philosophy of every person, every family for themselves. The welfare of ordinary individuals and families is at stake.

Women who had gone back to paid work in the seventies, entered the work force in the eighties, or had been working straight on through since World War II have been experiencing tremendous strain along with their husbands and families. By the nineties, the strain had not lessened. We entered the 21st century with most adults who were combining jobs with parenting still having a difficult time of it.

Old questions are being revisited. Now they need answers. In calling upon our ethical sensibilities and desire to strengthen families at their core, and utilize the gifts of everyone, we will find ways to see women and men as whole human beings combining the best of so-called "feminine" and "masculine" traits. We can make it easier for men and women to share in all forms of human work simultaneously if that is what they choose to do.

People in families are going to begin to assert themselves in concert, both to protect their own interests and to become advocates for a safer, less violent, less usurious, less militarized world. We are ready to protect human rights and the environment in which we all make a home.

In the context of the things that have gone before and the many things that are yet to unfold before us, living in the present moment we begin a discussion of the four basic forms of human work: housework, care-taking work, paid work, and volunteer work. We will explore how women and men can, do, and will share in all of them in spite of ideals, attitudes and practices that get in the way.

INTERLUDE

As we move on to look at work in its many forms, I want to share with you two fanciful children's stories that I loved when I was young. I think Ferdinand the Bull and the Country Bunny have something to say to us today as we contemplate our working lives. Take from the brief synopsis of these tales what you will.

FIRST, FERDINAND. FERDINAND was a bull who did not like to fight and butt heads the way the other bulls did. He liked to smell flowers. By a quirk of fate, Ferdinand was chosen to fight in the bull ring. Expectations were high as the Banderillos, Picadores, and the Matador entered the ring. Then came Ferdinand. When he saw the flowers in the hair of the lovely lady spectators he just sat down and sniffed. He ruined everything! They had to take him home. He saved his own life that day and who knows, maybe the life of the Matador too.

In the story of the Country Bunny, we find her, the mother of many children (as bunnies are wont to be) vying with strong jack-rabbits and fine white rabbits for the position of Easter Bunny. The old grandfather bunny, who is doing the hiring, chooses her because she is swift, wise, and kind. The grandfather, who is quite wise himself, asks her as she is standing in front of him with her offspring, how she can take on this task with so many children. As the story continues, it becomes clear that the mother bunny has organized her children well and they all do the housework together. And so it happened that the country bunny becomes the Easter bunny.

From the story of the Country Bunny and Ferdinand, I learned that bunnies and bulls can exceed common expectations. I also learned that our character and what we do with our lives are connected. Being kind, wise and organized was basic to everything in the country bunny's life. Being gentle, enjoying nature, and eschewing violence was central to Ferdinand's life. And these qualities were good things for each of them and the world around them.

Of course, we do not live in children's stories. But there are lessons to be learned from them.

CHAPTER 2

BEYOND GENDER POLARIZATION

So what is wrong with eating an apple?
Eve and Adam had no idea that what they were doing
Would change everything
On humanity's way to the tree of life.

WORK HAS A central place in our lives – all forms of work. We spend most of our adult waking hours working in many and varied ways. While some work we do comes with a pay check, some does not. We enjoy some, and find some a drag.

The four basic forms of work essential to life are: housework, paid work, family caretaking work, and volunteer work. Each has value though they are very different. Over the course of a lifetime, all of us will engage in several forms of work, often simultaneously.

Most of us do paid work in order to survive, and parenting work for the survival of our children. We do housework because we have to and volunteer work because we want to. Through our work we provide for shelter, food, medical care, education, entertainment. And through this work, we satisfy basic human needs for self expression, intimacy, and participation in human community.

Through our work we serve our own and society's needs. We are relational beings who are connected to one another and we depend on one another's labors for survival. We are social beings who order our lives in families, communities, institutions, and nations. We are interdependent people who derive meaning from and give meaning to one another. We affirm or deny, we value or disparage, we use or abuse each other's labors.

We are creators, giving birth to children and raising them. We make and discover things, care for and order them. We are artists. Thus, we express ourselves in multiple ways that emerge out of our physical, mental, emotional, and spiritual being. In multiple ways we participate in the making of history.

We are theologians, philosophers, myth makers. Our work is not only in our doing but in our thinking about who we are. The many ways in which we work and live have a great impact on who we are and are becoming, and how our world is evolving. The value we give to various forms of work matters.

As you read on, note that "gender" refers to being male or female in social context, implying the definitions society places on the sexes. One's sex simply refers to whether one is female or male. Patriarchy refers to the social system of organization in which men are the dominant sex and women's and men's life roles are separated.

WHO DOES WHAT WORK?

In the past, our society was organized in a patriarchal system that assumed male dominance and gender polarization. Gender polarization assigned women to two of the four kinds of work, housework and family work, and men to paid work, with women doing the bulk of society's volunteer work. Men and women were merged in marriage and each was the other's half. Because men were in the wider world, humanity was defined in male terms and "man" became the generic word for human. Men ran the world. Women kept the home and family running.

When the work of men and women is segregated by sex in this way, women and men actually live in separate life spheres, "women's world" and "men's world."

In a world in which women and men take on the work roles for which they are presumed to be most fit, certain characteristics are identified as belonging to women or men, "feminine" or "masculine" traits. Women are supposed to be relational and care about connection. They are nurturing, intuitive and spiritual. Men are supposed to be pragmatic and oriented toward justice. They are tough, decisive and objective. It is assumed that in the world of paid work, masculine traits are needed and in the work of the home, feminine traits are needed.

In a patriarchal system, women can cross gender lines if they do not marry, or if they do not have children. Men can cross gender lines in extreme emergencies. And married people with children who cross gender lines are exceptions at best and deviants at worst – or poor.

Today, this polarization is being reaffirmed by some political and religious leaders while others are challenging the gender dualism that underlies patriarchal systems. In the same year that Nancy Pelosi became the first woman to be Speaker of the House, Southwestern Baptist Theological Seminary instituted a course for women entitled, "Biblical Model for the Home and Family." The course is designed to enable women to perform their traditional feminine duties with excellence and grace and it is based on the following premises:

> "God values men and women equally, any student here will
> tell you. It's just that he's given them different responsibilities:
> Men make decisions, women make dinner."

Though there has been a tremendous revolution in women's and men's working roles, the changes that have come about still seem somewhat fragile. The "patriarchal system" and old stereotypes still lurk beneath the surface of our modern lives. Those things that have changed are often seen as economically (not philosophically) driven. We are to assume that eventually, either biology or religion or both will pull us back to reality

Sarah Palin, while Governor of Alaska and a candidate for Vice-President (both positions of power), was portrayed by her staff as a "Soccer Mom" with great empathy for "Joe Six-pack." These two stereotypical Americans are more than working class images, they are straight out of a system that relies on gender separatism as an operating principle. The contrast between the reality and the spin is stark, and to anyone paying attention, startling. Governor Palin left Soccer Mom in the dust awhile ago.

There were advantages in the old world view that continue to make it appealing. It was very clear. In this system, women and men knew who they were intended to be, how they were supposed to relate to one another, and what their life roles were supposed to be. And society knew who is supposed to do what and could order institutions accordingly. In the public realm, those who governed did not need to worry about the care of children.

In a family in which each person knew their place, life could run on automatic pilot. Husband and wife could be knit together in mutual dependency. This made the marriage bond seem strong, and marriages seem stable. But with men and women in their assigned places there were problems. Women had to lay to rest dreams of using their talents and gifts outside of their nurturing work, and they were economically dependent on men, leaving them vulnerable in the case of death, divorce, or abuse. Men developed a sense of political and sexual entitlement as a class and at the same time lived in hierarchical systems in which they were more often privates than generals. They engaged in society's physically demanding employment and most dangerous jobs.

Preparation for these gender stereotypes and roles began early. The individual talents of boys and girls were repressed if they did not fit the roles for which they were presumed to be most fit. Children were socialized for the adult roles for which their sex was presumed to suit them.

Clearly, within this system, many men and women built loving bonds in spite of gender limitations, sometimes because of them. As human beings we need intimacy and connection. We also want social approval and society tended to bless and reward those living within the patriarchal paradigm, making life easier for those who "fit in."

However, over time, patriarchy could not hold back the tide of change. Birth control enabled couples to have smaller families. Medical improvements led to extended life expectancy, and technology and the electronic age created a shift in the kind of paid work that is available in society. The Civil Rights Movement with its call for racial justice paved the way for a closer look at justice between the sexes.

Individuals became restless. In addition to the external challenges that were enabling us to expand gender roles, some interior psychological changes were taking place. Consciousness was being raised. In varying degrees, women and men began to embrace parts of their personalities and talents that had long been denied under stereotypical roles and expectations. Expanding gender roles and defying gender expectations began to seem appropriate and feel right.

Women were entering the workforce in record numbers, and entering fields once reserved for men. Men's lives were changing as they began to pick up some of the work at home, and entered fields once reserved for women. Finally it has become clear that worldviews held for centuries by people before us are being questioned and turned around. By now, the majority of women and men in the Unites States share, in one way or another, in all four forms of work.

On March 22 of 1998, the Washington Post ran a series of articles on Gender Roles written by Richard Morin and Megan Rosenfeld discussing the enormous shifts that have taken place in our working lives. They said:

> "A new national survey has found that after nearly a generation of sharing the workplace and renegotiating domestic duties, most men and women agree that increased gender equity has enriched both sexes. But both also believe that the strains

of this relatively new world have made building successful marriages, raising children and leading satisfying lives ever more difficult."

The responses collected in this study found some ambivalence in the respondents. While most of those surveyed approved of women's and men's changing roles, they found the strain of adopting this new life style difficult to live with. The fact is that ten years later gender equality continues to gain some ground. But the goal of breaking out of gender prejudices enough to make it easier for individuals to incorporate parenting and employment in their lives is still elusive.

Changing our life roles is not just about the structuring of women's and men's work roles in life. It is also about subtle and not so subtle assumptions, theologies, and philosophies about the nature of women and men, their relationships, and the ordering of societal and market life. The strain of evolving work roles affects us on a practical and emotional level. Until we develop new attitudes toward understanding gender roles, ambivalence will be a fact of modern life.

As we move beyond old paradigms, we know that there are things of value we want to take with us into the future. At the same time, we need to build the present and the future on premises and policies that differ from those of the past. We are changing the assumptions on which those premises were built. Changing assumptions lead to changes in our lives. Changes in our lives lead to changing assumptions. And in the entire process, what is happening in individual lives is intersecting with what is happening in our corporate lives. Change is taking place against the back-drop of the past.

Our forebears laid the groundwork on which we build in the present. While we know that slaves didn't believe in slavery, we cannot assume that most people who lived under patriarchy were unhappy about it. Nonetheless, something about their lives has brought us to this point in time. In living beyond gender polarization we are not betraying them, we are constructing a future they had begun to dream of.

In addition to being descendants of our own particular forebears, those in the Jewish, Christian or Muslim stream of life have two mythic forebears in common, Adam and Eve. Their story has helped define patriarchy. There is no need to assume that they are static role models. Perhaps they, like us, are on the verge of a new era, new assumptions, new practices, new social orders.

ADAM AND EVE

The Adam and Eve story in Genesis is the simplest, most elegant description of the male/female division of labor found in Scripture. Deeply embedded in culture, its influence has been pervasive. This is how the part of the story that is about work goes:

After Eve and Adam disobey God and eat fruit from the tree of the knowledge of good and evil, a curse befalls them in Genesis.

> God says to Eve: "I will greatly increase your pangs in child
>   bearing;
> In pain you shall bring forth children.
> yet your desire shall be for your husband,
> and he shall rule over you."
>
> God says to Adam: "Cursed is the ground because of you,
> In toil you shall eat of it all the days of your life,
> thorns and thistles it shall bring forth for you;
> and you shall eat the plants of the field.
> By the sweat of your face
> you shall eat bread
> until you return to the ground,
> for out of it you were taken;
> you are dust,
> and to dust you shall return."
>
> Genesis 3: parts of 14-19

Thus, at the beginning of the Bible, the basic dualistic premises of patriarchy were set down thousands of years ago and they persist as we know them today.

The "curse" placed on Adam and Eve describes a period in human history in which women and men have different missions in life. And during which time the female's desire will be for the male, who will rule over her. As for Adam, it seems that the specter of his mortality will rule over him.

But there is another creation story that puts the Adam and Eve story into perspective. In the first chapter of Genesis, our human origins are spoken of quite differently. In this story we catch a glimpse of an early theologian's vision of life before "the fall." Male and female are each created in the image of God, each is therefore in the other's image. Both are blessed by God and given responsibility to multiply, tend the earth and order it.

> "So God created humankind in his image;
> In the image of God he created them;
> male and female he created them." Genesis 1:27

On the surface, these could seem to be contradictory myths about creation. In fact, they make sense together. The story In Genesis 1 refers to our human potential, our original and universal state of being. The Adam and Eve story could refer to the beginning of a historic human era which seems like the beginning of time.

Eve and Adam, as prototypes of female and male, do not need to be locked forever at the beginning of time. They can enter another historic age, they can be rescued from being sentenced to gender polarization for all time. Our well being as human beings can involve both reclaiming our birth-right as created in the image of God, and going forward with our original forebears toward a societal order which enables us to express new truths about ourselves as we live into that image. As men and women, though there are differences between us, can it be that we are more alike than different as it says we are meant to be in Genesis 1? In the New Testament this truth is expressed in the statement that "in Christ there is neither male nor female"; we are all part of a "New Creation."

In the creation story in Genesis 3, sin enters the world. In the earlier story, all of creation is seen as good. We live with the tension of these two realities: creation is good and yet, as we try to live together spiritually and socially, we often fail, evil exists. Life is not perfect but we can move toward the greatest good, toward the light that remains in us. Absolute good is possible in God alone. Nonetheless, as human beings, the image of God remains imprinted on our souls.

Whatever "New Order" we are pressing toward, we will always live with limitations because we are finite beings, always part of the whole. I point this out to make clear that we are not searching for some utopian ordering of our working lives, or one way of living that is right for everyone as we proceed with our discussion of work. We are simply searching for ways in which we can move in hope toward ever better if still unfinished selves in the midst of a world still groaning to be free.

Adam and Eve were never meant to be static role models. They can never get back to Eden, from which they have been banned forever. They are well beyond the innocence and womb-like existence that would require. However, there is no reason to believe that the "curse" laid on them is permanent. As we look ahead with them, we see a tree of life in the future. They and we are meant to move on.

Today, we are poised for a major shift in worldview. Adam and Eve are ripe for liberation. While the Bible is written within the context of a patriarchal ordering of society, it gives us significant glimpses of life beyond this paradigm.

The seeds of any new order lie, at the very least, in extending the Ten Commandments to include women and strangers. With this in mind, our ethics can be built on taking seriously the summation of those Commandments, "To do to others as we would have them do to us," or to "Love God with heart, mind, and soul, and neighbor as self." Our closest neighbors are, of course, the ones with whom we live and work.

After Adam and Eve, Scripture does not give us one simple model for the ordering of home and family. In early stories in Hebrew Scripture, bigamy is acceptable, multiple wives are not a problem, nor is men's having children with slaves. By Jesus' time, monogamy seems to be the norm but without equality between men and women. Men could divorce their wives at will. One of Jesus' disciples is said to have exclaimed that if men cannot divorce their wives at their own discretion, what is the point of marriage?

We have to accept the fact that Scripture is not very specific about daily life in families. Scripture is, however, very clear that love and compassion are meant to be at the heart of our lives. We are left with the responsibility of finding ways to apply the ethical laws of love to our most intimate relationships as well as to the stranger. Over time, we have begun to change our ideas about love between women and men until finally we have asked whether patriarchy fosters that love. Of course, another basic question has nothing to do with love. It has to do with the turning of the wheels of society.

Our prototypical man and woman, Adam and Eve, can and do change over time as society seems to need: nothing to do with love. For a long time they changed without overturning the basic presuppositions inherent in the ancient myth and the patriarchal practices which followed. If we examine media images we can see the most recent variations of prototypical man and woman as they lead up to the present day. The media creates modern images, variations of Eve and Adam that stay, for the most part, within the structures of gender polarization. But, over time, cracks in that system begin to appear. Examining media images since World War 11 can be very revealing.

THE EVOLUTION OF ADAM AND EVE IN THE MEDIA

During World War II, men and women were encouraged to assume gender work roles to fit the needs of the time. Women were encouraged to work outside of the home while the men were away on the battlefront. When the war was over, women were supposed to return to their proper role as homemaker.

Rosie the Riveter and GI Joe were the patriotic prototypes for "Eve and Adam." Rosie was told to "man" the factories in men's absence and was assured that her children would thrive in Day Care. She could do any job a man could do. Anyone who could run a sewing machine could operate machines in a factory.

GI Joe was called to defend his country on the battlefield. He became a fighting man whose life was on the line for his country and whose heart was where the home fires were burning. He was needed to defend democracy and to make the world a safe place for those he loved. So when he was drafted to serve, he went willingly. Some women entered the armed forces with men and some men were conscientious objectors. Those who were too young or too old to be directly involved in the war effort supported it in different ways while Rosie and GI Joe remained the prototypical heroes.

When the GI Joes came home, Rosie was told to go home. Women had been filling in and doing "men's work" in a time of emergency. Now they could return to their "own work," housework and parenting. The clear message was that women's and men's work are different.

Rosie turned into Happy the Homemaker while GI Joe tried to settle down to become Successful. They moved to the suburbs and tried to create a beautiful home away from the problems of the world and the terrible memories of war. They wanted their children to grow up with green grass in the security GI Joe had earned.

Of course there were those who never moved to the suburbs or had beautiful homes. Those who were poor stayed behind in the cities. There were many women who continued to work and men who couldn't find work. But their lives were shrouded in silence. Behind the closed doors in both the suburbs and city, there was some unrest and in some homes, violence, addiction and despair. But the prevailing image was one of family satisfaction and contentment.

Some GIs had not come home. Others were physically or emotionally wounded. Mainstream America put on a happy face and turned toward the future. It would take more wars before the casualties of war would come into clear focus and the cost in human lives on all sides, civilian and military, would be more fully addressed. It has yet to be fully addressed.

It never occurred to us as a society to question the myths about work roles following the War. Happy the Housewife and Successful the up-and-coming Worker dominated media images. Men and women were creating secure homes and families by each doing their own work. The fixed message was that in spite of women's and men's changed work roles during the war, their right roles had now been resumed. Life had returned to normal. The war crisis was over and with it women's and men's response to it.

Successful Adam now had to make up for lost time spent on the battlefield and Happy Eve had to make a nest for her man who had come home. She had to give her full attention to caring for her children. Daycare centers that were in and praised during the war were now out. A responsible mother was certainly not ever going to send her children to day-care centers again.

As it turned out, Happy the Homemaker was not so happy after all. The door to another way of living had been opened. She was restless and often feeling trapped. The second wave of the Women's Movement was on the horizon.

Women were self consciously beginning to question their role and place in society, to identify the problems of patriarchy, to name the injustice of sexism, and to push beyond the confines of gender dualism, as they entered heretofore male professions and began to seek better day-care for all employed parents. And they began to notice the many mothers who had been in the workforce all along.

As the Women's Movement explored sexism and identified discrimination against women in society, Eve turned into Supermom. She could get out of her home if it made her happy. In fact, she could do almost anything. Supermom was a quick-change artist, wearing a suit to work, jeans at home, and a social dress to parties in the evenings. She could have it all and do it all. But she would soon wear herself out.

The message was clear: if she wanted to do other work along with her primary work of mothering, she could try, but mothering was still her primary work.

Successful continued in his career and fought off images of Embattled Man. Society's primary response to feminism, which men were expected to adopt, was to half-heartedly support women's equality in the market place for those women who had to work, as long as they continued to do the housework and parenting. There was little pressure on men to change their own life style. Media images seemed to encourage men to refocus their effort at work while trying to be supportive of women's new consciousness. The message that came across was that men and women were happiest in traditional relationships, even if women had to find employment to supplement the family's income – or, in some special cases, to satisfy their own vocational interests.

In mainstream America, men never got to address their own issues in a serious manner. While the majority of those in the Women's Movement did not see men as the "enemy," seeing sexism as a systemic problem, the media often seemed to encourage men to take the women's movement personally as a threat to their masculinity.

By now, the anti-Vietnam War Movement was in full swing. Men began to address the devastating effect war has on men in particular and on the whole human family. The Civil Rights Movement, the Anti-War Movement, the Women's Movement, and an emerging Gay Rights Movement, were all in motion. While not everyone participated in or agreed with the goals of these movements, they were affecting our national agenda.

Somehow, the Vietnam Vet became one face of Adam. He had gone to war and suffered immensely without becoming the Hero. Now, War itself was in danger of being challenged when our larger-than-life images took a huge turn. We were getting back to tradition and the ascendency of the upper classes.

Eve had theoretically entered a new era, a time of "Anything Goes" and "Whatever Works." She could wear high heels or clunky-funky flats. While Adam too had some new freedoms, he could wear gray flannel suits or jeans, he still had primary responsibility as breadwinner and public persona and defender of the nation while Eve continued to have primary responsibility for child care and housework, whatever else she chose to do. And the old images of men's and women's roles in life again seemed appealing.

As a result of the "Liberation Era" Adam could spend more time with his children, and Eve could earn money. But that was as far as either of them was supposed to go. An ad presents two images of a woman, one as a smart shopper at Sears and one as a doctor of biology. "Which of these two women," the ad asks, "is the intelligent one?" The right answer is that obviously the smart shopper is the more intelligent.

The message was clear. The values undergirding life were unchanged. Women were born to be homemakers and consumers. Women and men can go so far and no farther in challenging their traditional roles. Society is going to remain ordered on the old paradigm.

While religious conservatives were trying to hold the line on patriarchy, the media depicted Eve and Adam as pragmatic, materialistic people, doing what they had to do to survive. Then came a new twist: the connection between sexuality and "femininity" or "masculinity" was being asserted. Being "feminine" and "masculine" in a stereotypical sense came into vogue as crucial to being sensual and living a physically fulfilled life, having fun in the unsettling world of gender. We are in the era of Sex front and center in earnest.

The amazing thing is that so many men and women in the midst of these larger-than-life prototypes are living and have lived outside of them without much notice. Eventually, we all have to step back and ask ourselves whether or not we can be manipulated by current stereotypes. We really are free to define our working lives as women and men according to our own ethics and situations. Of course we live in the context of our society and will be affected by our cultural environment. However, we do not come as blank slates. We come with values and beliefs.

When we confront issues of sexism it can sometimes feel like being disloyal to past generations. Or it can simply feel like abandoning life styles or religious beliefs that worked. As a society, while we have been supportive of women's rights, we have stopped short of seeing where the deepest problems of patriarchy lie, those that prevent the real healing of our lives and our society. Some powerful ideologies are still in place. We live in a time when we are not just breaking out of old molds, we are engaged in breaking the molds and are in search of new ways of viewing life. Fortunately, the old molds are social constructs. We do not lose and will not be abandoned by the Universal Spirit that guides us and goes before us on our life journeys. We will not fall apart.

IDEAL IMAGES AND IDEOLOGIES

Over the centuries, our religious traditions have taken pragmatic patriarchal practices, even as they are changing, and called them God's will. Society has taken these practices and called them psychologically, biologically, and socially normative. Undergirding these practices and perpetuating them are idealized images and stereotypes about our identity as men and women and our working lives.

Ideal gender stereotypes and the structures of gender polarization reach the level of idolatry in society when these propositions are seen as essential tenets and cornerstones of a religious faith, or of civil religions, both of which see gender stereotypes as givens of human nature on which social systems are to be built.

When Gender Polarization becomes a prevailing ideology, it assumes the status of "Truth" that neither God nor Science could or ever would challenge. After all, God the Father and Mother Nature ordained life that way. Even in a society in which people's lives veer from the ideal, the ideal can retain its power. The ideal is buttressed by stereotypes and narrowly defined archetypes that help hold it in place. Values and worldviews that fly in the face of the "Truth" do emerge in individual and community life.

Katie Cannon in speaking about Black women's experience through the lens of literature, in *Womanism and the Soul of the Black Community*, refers to the power of archetypal stereotypes.

> The Black women's literary tradition provides a rich resource and a coherent commentary that brings into sharp focus the Black community's central values, which in turn frees black folks from the often deadly grasp of archetypal stereotypes. The observations, descriptions, and interpretations in Black literature are largely reflective of cultural experiences. They identify the frame of social contradiction in which black people live, move, and have their being. The derogatory caricatures and stereotypes ascribed to Black people are explicitly rejected. Instead, writings by Blacks capture the magnitude of the Black personality.

"The deadly grasp of archetypal stereotypes" about which Cannon speaks has a wide and universal reach, impacting all ethnic and racial groups. Racial prejudice needs stereotypes to buttress its control in society. So does gender prejudice. Archetypal stereotypes come in many guises. When dealing with gender issues, it is sometimes hard to distinguish negative images from positive ones. Stereotypes about women and men have a way of metamorphosing into ideal images.

The ideals of gender dualism have helped define "Motherhood," the "Ideal Worker," and an "Ideal Marriage" over the years. These ideals have shaped cultural expectations, and undergirded social structures in the past. They have seemed right and good. They still haunt our psyches and society today even as we live beyond these outmoded norms.

As we explore the four forms of work in the following chapters, we will identify the ideals related to them, explore how our experience veers from those ideals, and engage in the critical task of unmasking them and redefining our reality. We will face squarely the values inherent in the ideals, retain that which is of worth in them, and seek to replace them with our own deeply-longed-for values.

Many young people are liberating their minds from the bondage of gender role expectations and the "shoulds" and "oughts" that older generations have internalized, but age-old stereotypes are obstinate. No change we make in our personal and family lives will endure if we do not change the presuppositions that have held the old systems in place. We need to get to the root of the problems. In this pursuit, generations need to work together. When our beliefs and our actions are in harmony a new creation can begin to emerge.

The old separatist model that emphasized the differences between women and men and assumed different roles for the sexes may seem simplistic today, and very limiting as a blueprint for the future. Yet it still has power and shows up in various guises that lead to sexist thinking and acting.

When an ideological Truth that no longer holds meaning for society is allowed to remain in place and new ethical thought does not emerge, society can descend into chaos and free fall. We need to do more than diverge from the past, we need to consciously embrace new values.

John McCutcheon's song, "Water from Another Time," has a line in the chorus which says, "The old ways help the new ways come." We live in a time of transition. The "old ways" have things to teach us and we want to embrace the good inherent in them even as we reach for new ways of defining ourselves,

Society still seems to have an emotional attachment to the past. We need to know that we can claim all that is of value from it without buying into the whole traditional patriarchal paradigm. This is key to developing our own sustainable futures. The goal is to let go of stereotypes that have become crippling, to trust what we know to be real. We can participate in creating a social order that is more honest, more just, more whole, and more life giving. The ground has been prepared for us.

Right now, I sense that we are living beyond the old paradigms without challenging them outright. We are like the people who were afraid to acknowledge the fact that the Emperor had no clothes. We may try to hold on to past assumptions about gender identity and roles but they are as empty as the Emperor was naked. Still, we hesitate to say so.

The future is uncharted. Most of us are "flying by the seat of our pants." The new paradigms will have to emerge out of our lived experiences and mindfulness.

I don't think we can create a new myth. Myths evolve organically over great time spans. We can work to liberate our mythical Adams and Eves. We can replace old ideologies with new ethical imperatives that will set the foundation for new paradigms to emerge. We can affirm women and men as whole beings. We can pursue men's empowerment in the home as well as in the marketplace, and women's enfranchisement in the workplace as well as in the home, even as we support both men's and women's right to balance all forms of work in their lives as they see fit. We can affirm the importance volunteer work has in our lives and in society. We can support all children's development as both caring and productive adults. And we can democratize housework in the process.

In order to get beyond the old patriarchal paradigm which is based on the significance of the inherent differences between women and men, we have to explore the relevance of those differences in today's world.

GENDER DIFFERENCES: BIOLOGY AND CULTURAL ENGINEERING

From the beginning, let us state the obvious: women can bear children and men cannot, though a few transgendered men have done so. And, with rare exceptions, women can nurse babies and men cannot. The issue is how much this matters in our working lives in today's world. Gerder Lerner, in *The Creation of Patriarchy*, sees gender as a "status difference."

> "In addition to age, gender is one of the universal dimensions
> on which status differences are based. Unlike sex, which is
> a biological concept, gender is a social construct specifying

the socially and culturally prescribed roles that men and women are to follow."

Wilma Scott Heide, a sociologist and leader in the Women's Movement and twice President of NOW, argued along with other sociologists, psychologists, and civil rights activists, that there are no differences between women and men that are significant enough to justify a gender-defined separation of women and men. These apologists argue that differences between the sexes do not need to track our life trajectories, defining prescribed life roles.

To understand ourselves and our work roles, the important question to ask is how physiological differences between women and men effect women's ability to work for pay outside of the home and men's ability to do work at home over the course of a lifetime. Are the differences between men and women significant enough to support a social system that prepares and tracks men and women into different work roles: that assigns them stereotypical characteristics that fit those roles, and relegates them to cultural "worlds" accordingly?

The interesting thing is that whether or not one believes in the importance of gender differences between women and men does not always correlate with how they live their lives.

Driving home from a family gathering, we were listening to a CD. The book was "*The Female Brain*." I was fascinated and impressed with the author's discussion about girls' adolescent sexuality and found it interesting and informative. I became a little concerned when at one point in her analysis she declared women unstable at certain times of the month: I wondered if we were to assume that women are not therefore fit for public leadership. Then she talked about male sexuality and the number of times boys and men have sex on the brain, and I wondered about male fitness for leadership. I concluded that women and men both have hormonal issues with which to cope when they are at work in the world.

When Louann Brizendine got to discussing the "Mommy Brain," I began to have trouble with her analysis. She did not really specify how long this "Mommy Brain" lasts as it takes over a woman's psyche and senses. I wondered if a "Daddy Brain" exists on some level. By the time she got to women's change of life, she was acknowledging that women change over the course of a lifetime.

Susan Pinker in *The Sexual Paradox* is also interested in differences between boys and girls. She focuses primarily on the special needs many boys have that need to be addressed in our educational systems. She sees girls as more adept when it comes to learning. However, in spite of these differences, she says:

> "There is no biological evidence that women should stay home and raise babies. Nor is there proof that men and women are indistinguishable, and with the same opportunities, will value the same things and behave the same way. Instead the data reveal a handful of different catalysts for people's choices – many with neurological or hormonal roots, and others that reflect workplaces designed to meet the male standard – that mesh to create the real gender gap."

Caryl Rivers and Rosalind C. Barnett, writing for the Boston Globe, entitle their article, "The Difference Myth." They debunk the "scientific" writing on brain differences between girls and boys as bad science and a way to "shore up some of society's most unscientific prejudices."

The discussion about differences between the sexes is certain to be ongoing given our recent social past which segregated women's and men's work. Sorting out biology from gender experience and cultural engineering is almost impossible. There are bound to be differences between men and women, and boys and girls, which developed out of their social context along with differences which are physiologically given.

While thinking about the differences and similarities between women's and men's physiology, I picked up a newspaper and read about a woman's heart being transplanted into a man's chest. That helped the discussion on differences between the sexes fall in place for me. Our sexual organs are one part of our anatomy, and that part of our anatomy accounts for many differences between the sexes. There is, however, all the rest of our anatomy. The heart that makes everything else tick is interchangeable between women and men. The similarities between women and men may be more important than the differences in the long run. Women and men share a common humanity.

Looking at the overall evidence of lived lives, there do not seem to be any differences between men and women that justify keeping women out of the paid work force or eliminating men from housework and the care of children. Nor are there any differences which justify women's subordination to men in society. Theories about sexual differences abound but they do not all lead to the support of traditional gender roles.

Against the backdrop of all intellectual discussions is the reality of our lived lives.

OUR WORKING LIVES SPEAK FOR THEMSELVES

The fact is, that even though we have conditioned women and men for traditional roles, enough women and men have, against the odds, broken out of their assigned gender identities for us to know that those identities and the roles and the character traits that presumably accompany them are more forced than real. We can even come to the conclusion, taking a close look over time, that there is a correlation between gender roles and class roles. Typical gender roles have been applied most consistently to mainstream, middle class, men and women.

We have biographical evidence of many people crossing traditional gender lines over time – some without society's blessing and some with it, some out of necessity and some out of choice – or privilege.

As a Minister I have experienced first hand the crossing of professional gender lines along with my clergy colleagues and many in other helping professions. When I was first ordained, I was entering a profession understood as male. On the other hand, male clergy have often been seen as having "feminine" gifts. In fact, clergy have sometimes been identified as a "third sex."

When I was in Seminary students took a psychological test to determine their suitability for ministry. *The Strong Preference Test* had a masculinity and femininity index. As might be expected I tested a little over on the masculine side and many of my male colleagues came out a little on the feminine side. We worried about this some, but ended up basically dismissing it. Were we all deviant or were we simply well rounded?

Women in the sciences have given evidence that women can do science, a traditionally male subject. A recent study has shown that girls have closed the gender gap with boys in math. Both male nurses and female doctors have entered professions once reserved for the other sex. I no longer make note of it when a man answers as a telephone operator, or when the surveyor who comes to mark the boundaries of our property is a woman. I may still notice when the person pushing a baby carriage is a man, but I do not think it strange. When a heterosexual couple brings a potluck dish to a meeting I can no longer assume the woman made it. None of the people who are living beyond traditional gender roles are biological or social deviants.

Friends of ours, a married lesbian couple, were raising a niece and a nephew and had to decide how to divide up work between them without gender roles to either guide or sidestep. They decided that Lisa who was an architect would be the primary bread winner, and Sally who was an artist would take primary responsibility for housework and parenting while she worked on her art at home.

In some ways, raising the question of biology and destiny comes too late when it comes to our working lives. It is moot. Biology is not destiny according to how we are already living, nor is it so according to how many in past generations have lived theirs.

ECONOMIC REALITY AND EXPANDED GENDER ROLES

Men and women of all races and ethnic identities who were fighting an uphill economic battle have often had to live outside gender stereotypes in order to survive. They have combined all forms of work in their daily lives out of necessity. Husbands and wives have both held jobs to make ends meet, not having the luxury of living a totally sexually polarized lifestyle. For many immigrant and minority men and women, prescribed gender roles were for the well-to-do. Gender dualism was an ideal beyond reach that the privileged enjoyed.

While many women who were also mothers were indeed working outside of the home over the years, this did not inevitably lead to equality. Professor Sang Hyun Lee, writing in 1995, said:

> "Much of the economic success of many Asian immigrants is due to the inordinate amount of labor provided by women at business places. But women do not enjoy the same status and privileges as men either at home or in the church."

Women were the ones who most often embraced all forms of work, being employed and caring for the family. Among those struggling economically, men often held two jobs or worked long hours. Men more often than women faced the devastations of unemployment or were absent from the family, off in search of survival. But in some homes, men did all forms of work alongside of women without any public recognition or support.

There were also single parents, most of whom were women but some of whom were men, who combined all four forms of work in order to survive. My paternal grandmother and aunt supported their families after their husbands died as did many other women in that coal mining region.

One of the African American women we spoke with in our early survey was the daughter of a single mother who had raised five children. She had become a lawyer herself and was a single mother raising three children. She said, "When I was growing up, it never occurred to me to imagine myself dependent upon a man. I always assumed I would work and my husband would too. That was just the way it was." No white middle class norm there.

At the other end of the spectrum, the super rich have always been able to live outside of many of the norms established for the middle class. They could hire help, send their children to private school, and create their own culture. That did not automatically mean parity in gender relationships. It did mean freedom from some gender role responsibilities for both women and men.

As economic times change, more middle class families are in a position to identify with and learn about survival and sharing work roles from those who have lived beyond stereotypes over the course of time. Living outside of gender norms may have been difficult at times, but it was not unnatural. We can admire the strength and the coping skills of those who have had to define themselves. More and more middle class families are following in their footsteps, as class lines, except for the very poor and the very rich, are blurring.

With the work choices we make and the work realities we are faced with come satisfactions and stresses in whatever kind of work we do. We can remember that both satisfaction and stress come from many causes, economic, emotional, spiritual, and physical. And each form of work, whether it be parenting or other employment, comes with its own built-in stressors. Women can't resolve work-related stress by returning to traditional work roles and patterns, and men can't resolve work-related stress by pursuing gender roles with greater vigor. The work from which we derive greatest fulfillment is not determined by our gender. We all derive our realization in multiple forms of work and experience strains in those activities as well.

RECOGNIZING INDIVIDUAL DIFFERENCES

Individuals differ widely from one another within the same gender group. All women are not alike. All men are not all alike. Sometimes we forget this. Society has many ways of measuring differences between people that do not rely on gender.

For instance, we have Myers-Briggs categories to understand ourselves and one another: introverted and extraverted, feeling and thinking, intuitive and sensate, perceptive and judging. Or we have Eneagram types. We have childhood experiences and family patterns that help form our character. Or sometimes society divides us into categories based on group identity other than gender such as race, ethnicity, nationality, religion, age, sexual orientation. Add to the mix, physical differences and genetic variations.

Categorizing ourselves and others is fascinating and sometimes useful if it gives us insights into ourselves and our human condition. Seeing ourselves and one another through these lenses can also be limiting if not dangerous. We are persons beyond all the categories we can come up with. We are human beings beyond any narrow definition of ourselves.

Whatever gender and developmental differences we live with, we are all individuals who do not fit into boxes. This is not to say that our group identities do not matter. They help to make us who we are. When we come together in relationships and create new families, form social networks, and enter the world of employment, we bring all of our differences and complexities with us. We also bring our unique character and our common humanity. To the extent that gender matters, it does not need to determine our working lives.

SEEKING COMMON VALUES IN OUR WORKING LIVES

Since our gender need not determine the kind of work we are fit for as women and men, we ask a different question. Does the kind of work we do call on and develop different capacities in those who do it? Do different skills lead to different values?

On the face of it, parenting develops relational skills and a deep regard for connection. Employment in the wider world turns our attention toward achievement, and ultimately, justice.

Studies on moral development in males, conducted by Lawrence Kohlberg, pointed to their keen sense of justice and objective way of viewing the world. Carol Gilligan, following up on his work, studied female development, and found relationship to be a core value for women. Jean Baker Miller, like Carol Gilligan, saw connection as being of central importance to women in whatever work they undertook.

Initially it seems that men and women bring different gender-based gifts to the work they do. However, both Gilligan and Miller speculate that these different gifts could be more dependent on life roles and social systems than on biology. Miller imagines a time when the gifts of women are utilized in the public realm and the gifts of women and men are joined, leading to greater human development and social maturity. She writes of this vision in *Women's Growth in Connection:*

> "I believe that the search for the more appropriate study of women in women's own terms can not only lead to understanding women; certainly a valid goal in itself, but can also provide clues to a deeper grasp of the *necessities* for all human development, and simultaneously, to a greater realization of the realities and the vast untapped human capacities. This is not an easy thing to do, because our whole system of thought, our categories, the eyes with which we see and the ears with which we hear have been trained in a system removed from this activity."

Picking up on our universal need for relationship, Archie Smith says in *The Relational Self: Ethics and Therapy from a Black Church Perspective,* "Personal morality and individual reality are embedded in, and continue to emerge from, the web of dynamic relations which constitute it. In Boesak's proverbial words, 'One is only human because of others, with others, for others.'"

Smith is pointing to the fact that we all live in a web of relationships that define who we are as human beings. The same point was made by Ivan Nagy, Barbara Krasner, and Margaret Cotroneo in a Continuing Education Symposium at Harvard Divinity School on Relational Dynamics and Theology. They not only affirmed the given importance of relationship in our lives, but the givenness of our drive toward reciprocal justice in the context of connection.

Clearly, the gifts men and women bring to whatever work they do are enhanced when connection and justice are valued together and are of central importance in our system of values.

As our gender roles become more fluid, we can dream with Jean Baker Miller and others that we are moving toward a time when "vast untapped human capacities" can be unleashed.

Wilma Scott Heide, playing with our so-called "feminine/masculine" traits, developed ways they could be unified to become transcendent qualities in individuals that serve the good of society as a whole. Here is a sampling of her list.

"Feminine"	*Transcendent*	*"Masculine"*
affective	discerning	cognitive
microcosm	universal	macrocosm
dependent	interdependent	independent
intuitive	knowing	rational
care	curative care	cure
feeling	being	thinking
emotional	existential	intellectual
body	self/human	mind

She invites readers, as I do, to make their own lists and imagine transcendent qualities for themselves. Combining the best characteristics once assigned to us as female and male holds great hope for our future and the future of religion and society.

Patricia Martin Doyle, a student of Erik Erikson, developmental psychologist, and of Paul Tillich, theologian, writes about their vision of a time when the traits once assigned by gender are blended. In an Essay in a book edited by Rosemary Radford Ruether, *Religion and Sexism*, she says:

> "Both "masculine" and "feminine" elements are transcended as they are combined in a new "mix." One can imagine men and women living in the Spiritual Presence and the Spiritual Community who are able to unite within themselves and their culture the previously warring alternatives of separate male or female consciousness alone. I believe such a consciousness is

prophetic of our future, that a new era awaits realization, in which the promises of Galatians 3:28 may be fulfilled, that 'There is neither Jew nor Greek, there is neither slave nor free, there is neither male nor female, for you are all one in Christ Jesus.'"

As men and women share in all forms of work, we learn from one another. Defying stereotypes and expectations in matters both simple and profound, we dare to define our own way of being and working, pursuing our deeply held values. We can imagine some shared values: seeking peace and abhorring violence in our homes and world, cherishing children, being creative in employment, exercising conscience, cleaning up the environment at home and in the world, joining together in volunteer work in the arts and in service to the community.

The values and ethical positions we hold dear as human beings come from our hearts and minds, our whole being, not our genitals. The sexes are equal in their capacity to reject values that destroy life and to hold fast to values that are life-giving.

BASIC VALUES IN OUR WORKING LIVES

So, we return to Eve and Adam and all of us who are their heirs. After years and years of living with gender polarization and male dominance as the norm in the United States, the past fifty years have opened the door for change. We step out into an emerging New Creation, far from Eden, and move toward the ultimate, the Tree of Life. Our universal pair now have many descendants who are diverse and different from one another, each harboring the original light and spark of creation, each with a capacity for wholeness and intimacy.

Some of the marks of the new creation are clear. Others are yet to be discovered and uncovered. Where men and women were once seen as each other's half, complete only when male and female joined in procreation, we can now see each person is created for wholeness, complete in the image of God.

Clearly, Adam and Eve were joined by mutual need and dependence. Today, in our individual wholeness we are joined interdependently, by affection and commitment and faithfulness. Women and men, once assigned to separate roles in life, can now share in all forms of human work, having responsibility in the home and the world, bringing these worlds closer together. This gives future generations more options.

As women and men become partners with neither ruling over the other they realize new opportunities for cooperation and harmony and personal growth in the family. By dint of circumstance or human choice, some families will consist of a single parent. Some families will have two adults and no children. Some families will include three generations. Each person will be changing and developing over time.

We have not yet spoken of the nature of the God who demanded absolute obedience in the Garden of Eden and who banished Eve and Adam from paradise. Perhaps that God was never the Patriarch people made him out to be. Being banished from the Garden was, after all, the beginning of human freedom. It was a birthing. And God, over time, continued to be in relationship with humanity in a multiplicity of manifestations. And ultimately, in different religious traditions.

Over time, the God of Jews, Christians, and Muslims, referred to in male terms and carrying more "masculine" than "feminine" characteristics in mainstream religion, has begun to be seen through new spiritual eyes in many quarters.

Carrie Doehring, in *The Practice of Pastoral Care: A Post Modern Approach*, says this:

> "Gender has been a controversial issue for Christian traditions in the past fifty years. Those in a reconstructing mode challenge the patriarchal aspects of religious tradition, especially in terms of women's role in the family and the ordained ministry of the church. The move from male-dominated to gender-inclusive images of God also involves

a radical change from centuries-old doctrines and practices in which God was singularly identified as male.

"Generally speaking, a conserving orientation is part of premodern and modern approaches to knowledge in which theological propositions are true in all times and places. A postmodern approach to knowledge assumes that knowledge about God must be continually constructed to be relevant in complex historical contexts."

The evolution of our understanding of ourselves as human beings and our understanding of the Divine are intertwined. When we are pursuing changes in women's and men's roles this has a profound affect on our perception of and relationship with God. That is not to say that traditional insights about God have no place in our contemporary lives. However, it leaves the door open for the Holy's ongoing revelation of Self in our midst as we explore new possibilities for our human selves. God accompanies us on our journeys toward wholeness. On this journey, God reflects our multifaceted selves back to us and in turn we discover the many amazing facets of God. And we are complete as God is complete.

We change through the political and social movements of our time, the economic ups-and-downs. And over time with that change come philosophical and theological shifts. For human beings, to live is to change. Even our dreams and visions change. As we proceed to look at the four forms of work in our lives, we will discover ways in which our social systems also change to fit who we are and who we want to be, no matter what our cultural context or family configuration.

Perhaps, many of us would just as soon live our lives without thinking about change or these abstractions. We just want to be left alone to live our lives in peace. We don't care about the larger scheme of things. However, like it or not, we all affect our world and future generations by the way we order our lives around the work we do, and by the way we think about how we "ought" to be ordering our lives. We are setting the agenda for the future. We might as well pay attention.

Having new work and life options entails more choice and offers more possibilities. It requires more reflection on our part and a more deliberate identification of our values. In the chapters that follow, we will try to unmask old world views, explore new ways of perceiving ourselves, our relationships, and our work.

Our discussion will focus on men and women in families who are parents. This is because stereotypes and models apply most directly to this family structure. Our primary focus will be on middle class families as they are the ones on whom stereotypes fall most heavily.

Let it be noted, however, that people live in all kinds of family situations and I write with this in mind. Whatever their make-up, all families are affected by "norms and standards" set for the "typical" American family. This book is for heterosexual couples and homosexual couples, it is also for single parents, single adults, couples without children, couples with children, people in step-families, who all live in a society that has been structured to fit what was seen as the Ideal Family. As we deconstruct limiting stereotypes and reach for new ways of being in the world, we will all benefit.

THE VISION

We are reaching for a new vision that can embrace our current reality: new ethics, new boundaries, different ways of ordering society, deeper encounters with Divinity. We come seeking meaning for our lives.

Individuals and families have the right to choose working patterns that fit their own proclivities, needs, and economic realities. Society, for its part, can no longer assume polarized roles for women and men. Some families will choose to live in traditional gender patterns that are no longer normative for everyone. In other families people will engage in all forms of work either simultaneously or serially. The burden of old gender ideals and stereotypes is being lifted for everyone.

This is about our dreaming together about what we want, not only for ourselves, but for the future, for our children and grandchildren and the society in which they will be living.

In my weaker moments, I have to wonder if what I want for future generations is a more simple life in which they are told who they are, are told what they are supposed to do, and don't have to make complicated and demanding choices. Let the girls be girls and the boys be boys. Why not hold on to patriarchy?

I know better. I know that that is not fair or desirable. That image of life is an illusion. Girls and women have dreams about work outside of the home as well as in it. Boys and men value intimacy and want to be good husbands and fathers. Human development drives us in the direction of wholeness, of creativity and vocation, of connection and nurturing. Spirituality and ethics drive us in the direction of abundant life, of industry and relationship, of autonomy and love, of justice and grace.

Gender polarization is a cornerstone of sexism and a critical component of the subordination of women to men in marriage and of men to unrestrained hierarchies in the marketplace. That is no longer a viable way to live. It is not fair to men or women. The dream is to move beyond patriarchy. I see in this dream the movement of the Spirit.

Being a Christian, I wonder about Jesus' position on the matter of work roles for men and women and this dream. Jesus did not make any definitive statements on divinely ordered work roles for women and men. In fact, Jesus never had to combine raising a family with his career, as far as we know. There is no text in which specific directions are laid out in Scripture for allocating work by gender once we get past Adam and Eve.

Jesus simply called everyone to do God's work regardless of gender. Jesus called people to wholeness, to washing each other's feet, to welcoming children, to healing, to plying their trade, to sharing the fruits of their labors, to multiplying their talents, to providing for everyone's basic needs, all in the service of the whole creation, all in a spirit of love, always paying attention to "the least of these."

Every religious tradition has its prophets, texts, and authorities that help us catch a vision for the future. We don't have to fit our rounded lives into the square holes of our social myths and structures. Together we can seek out streams of living water that bring us closer to the fullness of life. As we begin our discussion of each form of work we can be assured that all will be well

"The new American family is alive and well.

"Both partners are employed full time, and according to the latest research, the family they create is one in which all members are thriving, often happier, healthier, and more well-rounded than the family of the 1950s.

"That's the message of this new, myth shattering study of such couples, funded by a 1 million-dollar grant from the National Institutes of Mental Health."

This quote comes to us from *She Works/He Works: How two-Income Families are Happier, Healthier, and Better Off*, by Rosalind C. Barnett and Caryl Rivers.

We are moving toward life styles that lead to greater reciprocity and respect between men and women, and by extension, a greater compassion between all people and a greater reverence for life. It would be arrogant to believe that we are "starting from scratch." The past has paved the way for us. It is our job to move on.

CHAPTER 3

HOUSE WORK/HOMEMAKING

Life is not just about the big times
The daily details are what
Manage to float our boats.

Housework is a fact of
life. Everyone alive either
has to do it, get another family member to do it, or pay to have it
done. Housework has to do with the basics of life: caring for the roof
over our heads, buying, gathering, cooking food to eat, caring for the
clothes we wear and a myriad of other tasks related to daily living.

Work around the house is the first work we can learn to do.
Children can do it along with adults. By the time my grandchildren
were three they could help out with chores such as setting and clearing
the dinner table and picking up their toys.

Some philosophers see physical labor as a great equalizer and
something every citizen should experience. Housework is the most
universal form of physical labor there is and could be the greatest
work equalizer of all. It is not productive work, but without it, no

productive work could take place. This form of work which enables the productive worker's performance of duties is part of the productive economic cycle. Wherever you go in the world you will find people doing housework. It is a discreet form of labor.

Throughout my own growing-up years, and well into my adulthood, I had a negative attitude about housework and was ill prepared to do it. In my mind, it was most definitely an inferior form of work, repetitive, boring, and yet strangely beyond my competence. I wasn't interested in being good at it. My education in housework was minimal. My mother and grandmother kept the house running. I did dishes (or got out of doing them by telling my younger siblings bedtime stories), I did get good at ironing on the mangle, and I could cook an occasional meal. I got most of my housework training in my teen years when my grandmother was gone and my mother was hospitalized on several occasions. My husband who lived in dorm rooms from the time he was fifteen was even less prepared for housework than I was.

Going through some of my old papers, I found the following, a little pathetic, but revealing. My diary, November 1958.

> "If I ever have enough money to pay someone to help with our housework I shall regard whoever does it with a great deal of respect. The whole problem of running a house, while I suppose it will get somewhat easier, baffles me.
>
> "Take the other day. I woke up in the morning to tend to a crying baby (without enough sleep which never starts the day off well.) I came downstairs to find a hungry husband. On the surface of it, not difficult problems to solve. The baby, who was still crying, would soon have his bottle (sweet peace,) and my husband and I would have breakfast. To complicate things, however, I discovered that there were no clean clothes for the baby. I can't understand how that happened! So, in a surge of energy, I threw some clothes in the wash, put on a bottle to heat up, and eggs in a pot

to boil. Things were underway. As I stood there wondering what to do next, I heard a splashing sound. I opened my sleepy eyes a little wider and saw water gushing all over my kitchen floor. I had forgotten to put the washer hose in the sink. It is easier to remember Latin verbs. Everything was already soaked by the time I lunged for the hose and put it in the right place. The baby was amused by this activity and stopped crying. Just as I was contemplating what to do with the mess, my keen sense of smell tracked down a burning odor. The eggs! The milk in the bottle was much too hot of course. The baby began to cry again. My husband came to the rescue. He waded through the water (which later would be tracked on the rugs) to the sink to cool off the bottle, asking how I could manage to create such a mess. Soon the baby was being fed and while he was still, I tackled the floor. When I was finished, I had several buckets of dirty water which I dumped outside, which left me holding a dirty mop. I decided to rinse out the mop in the tub upstairs. (No bathroom downstairs.) I put the mop under the faucet in the tub and turned on the water. Down it came on my head. I was drenched. Which one of us had forgotten to turn the shower thing-a-ma-jig back up?"

This sounds pretty sad now. When I was first married, I was better at writing a sermon than keeping house, but keeping house was my job at that point. My husband was the breadwinner. Furthermore, I had bought into the concept of the "Ideal Housekeeper" even though I was totally unprepared for that role. Cleaning up one thing always seemed to lead to making something else dirty in an endless cycle of frustrating activity. After each meal was cooked there was the next one to think about.

Most often, women have been the ones to be doing daily chores around the house. They were supposed to live into the image of the good housekeeper.

THE IDEAL GOOD HOUSEKEEPER

In the ideal family, the Good Housekeeper was the "woman of the house" who was at the center of family activity. She was usually a Mother and the queen bee around whom home life revolves. She was fixed at the center of domestic life while other family members come and go. It was her job to create a comfortable home and run it. She was supposed to be a detail person who took care of the basic essentials of daily living so men and growing children, especially boys, could take care of more important matters, like earning money or preparing to do so.

In ideal homes, the Good Housekeeper ran the family for the comfort of the father. And when he was there, he was boss. The household was to be run the way he wanted it without his lifting a finger. He was doing the really important work of supporting the family financially and deserved the best of what the family had. He earned it.

Over time, the image of the Good Housekeeper shifted a bit as women gained more power in the home. The housekeeper had increasing say on practical matters. The kitchen in particular was hers, she knew where everything was and how to use it. And she decided what the family would eat.

The wife catered to her husband when he was there, but ran things her own way when he was absent and secretly enjoyed those times. "When the cat's away . . ."

Women were taught to see their homes as extensions of their own physical person. An unkempt home was a cause for shame. On the other hand, it was rather masculine for a young man's room to be a mess or for male dorms to be disaster areas. That was an expression of masculinity.

For the Good Housekeeper, godliness, sexual purity, and cleanliness were yoked. Dishes that sparkled became a face that shone. Ring around the collar was a sign of a messy, unkempt person. Soft wash was associated with soft skin. Media hype promoted these and many other images.

The Housewife was unpaid. Her work was a work of love. Being supported and loved by a husband and appreciated by her children was a wife's compensation. Women, it was supposed, enjoyed this kind of work. They did it by choice. They were, after all, cut out for it.

In the ideal, a housewife took pride in her husband's and sons' paid work and lived vicariously through them. She expected her daughters to follow in her footsteps. If a woman had young children, caring for them and the house was a full-time job. As the children got older, she had more leisure time and could engage in Volunteer Work in the community. If there was enough money in the family, another woman could be paid to do housework, which freed her for more social and charitable work.

In this image of the Ideal Homemaker, ideal husbands took care of fixing things that broke, were good at working with cars, kept up with outside work and oversaw major home repairs.

REALITY

The ideal is an illusion. If women do housework, it is not because they are uniquely fit for the job, or because they can do it so well, or as an act of love. Housework has quite simply been seen as women's work. Until recently, even if women worked outside of the home for pay they were expected to do the bulk of housework.

While the ideal Housekeeper is hard to find these days, the fact is that many women still do much of the housework in families, sometimes willingly, sometimes resentfully. For some, there is something satisfying about being at the center of family life. Others are more than willing to share that position. Still other women want to remain at the center of family life and have men do half of the household work.

When the Women's Movement was in full swing, the concept that women were cut out for housework was challenged. Some people referred to housework as "shit work" because they thought it represented women's servitude in the family and society.

Housework, in spite of the ideal that society tried to attach to it, was work which was done by slaves and then servants in well-to-do households. Women did their own housework when they couldn't pay someone else to do it. Class issues as well as gender and race issues entered the picture. Housework was work that was in reality perceived as beneath the rich and white men.

In poorer families, doing all of the housework while simultaneously earning money jeopardized women's health. Marcia Guttentag, doing research at Harvard University, discovered that women in low-paying full-time jobs, mothers of small children and wives of uncooperative husbands, doing all the housework, experienced such great stress in their lives that they had very high levels of depression and suicide.

In spite of these facts, some women who do not have to deal with economic stress say they enjoy housework and say they willingly choose this as their primary form of work along with parenting.

Our society has given women double messages about housework. On the one hand it put women whose primary work was housework on a pedestal and claimed to honor the Good Housekeeper highly. From a religious perspective, we elevated the Servant Image when the servant was a woman. But then, in many subtle and not so subtle ways, society made it clear that this work did not have much worth. Anyone who could avoid it, did. Women were given a "mixed message." Society masked discrimination against women with positive ideals.

How do we demystify the ideal, honor the women who did housework, and the people who do it today? How do we truly appreciate the work of maintaining a home and providing for the physical needs of family members? Most importantly, how do we involve all members of the family in this form of work, and still recognize the fact that some of it is and will always be plain physical labor?

HOMEMAKING

In the Women's Movement, while some were debunking housework, others were upgrading it to Homemaking. Homemaking was not only about chasing dirt, it was about nurturing the family, engaging in domestic arts, creating a safe, attractive, and friendly environment for living, creating a sanctuary, a nesting place of comfort and warmth:

good food, good company, good times. Being a Homemaker was an honorable profession . . . but, again, somewhat idealized.

The reality was that housekeeping and homemaking were different aspects of the same work. Some women liked doing them, some didn't. Some liked parts of homemaking and hated housework. Some women were willing to do basic housework but had no interest in domestic art.

I have had an epiphany since the early years of my marriage. While I don't totally reject all of my former attitudes about housework, I have come to appreciate the importance of housework, know that it is indeed real work and that it includes domestic arts which can enrich life. Housework, homemaking, goes a long way toward holding human life together. And the state of one's home can affect and reflect the state of one's heart and mind.

Whatever we call it, this form of work has a value to us as human beings that should not be underestimated. However, it is also a form of work able to be done by any household member who is not disabled. Men and children can do it as well as women.

HOUSEWORK AND JUST LOVE

In very fundamental ways, the home is a learning ground for human relationships and the ways in which we value and support or denigrate one another. In homes where traditional roles are played out, if those who are being served feel entitled to be waited on, there is an imbalance of justice. Those who are serving are learning their social "place" not only at home, but in the world. Those being waited on deserve this service because they are men and meant to be bread winners. This economic reality gives them a position of dominance in the home if they choose to exercise it.

As more women entered the workforce and also became breadwinners the balance of power began to shift. Initially men did not pick up on doing work at home. But over time, men and children have begun to share this work with women, putting love into action.

The allocation of house work among family members is a political issue with ethical, spiritual overtones. Saying "I love you," in families includes acting out that love in a fair division of labor in the home.

When we did our initial study of employed mothers in the late 1970s, women expressed anger about how unfair it seemed to them to have to work all day in the marketplace and then come home and work another shift at home. Their anger was coupled with exhaustion. How, women mused, could my husband love me when he is willing to sit around and watch me wear myself out without lifting a hand?

In two parent homes, if one member of the household is the primary breadwinner, then a different dynamic is at work. The one who by mutual choice stays at home, may well take on the bulk of the work at home and be economically entitled on an equal basis.

Increasingly, however, as more women share the work of earning money for the family, more men are picking up their share of the work at home (as children are where their age permits). We are reaching a point in our society's life when house work is increasingly being democratized. And the consensus is that most marriages are better for it.

Ann Oakley, writing in *The Sociology of Housework*, found that women's satisfaction with the amount of work men do at home was related directly to their satisfaction or dissatisfaction with their marriage.

Neil Chethik, in *VoiceMale*, writes, "Today, the division of household work stands as a potent marital issue. In the VoiceMale Survey, household responsibilities ranked third on the list of topics most likely to cause marital discord (behind only money and balancing paid work and family.) . . . . According to my survey, *those couples who work out a fair division of household duties have more frequent sex, are less likely to seek marriage counseling or consider a divorce, and are more happily married overall.*"

In addition to democratizing housework, families are utilizing outside resources as they can, professional, market, familial or social services. Companies who do housework professionally have sprung up and wages for those who make a living providing these services have increased. In families who can't afford to hire out parts of housework, or choose not to, take-out restaurants, including fast food chains, and prepared foods in the grocery store, are helping make life easier. Neighbors and family members share inside and outside household chores.

How families address the basic day-by-day tasks involved in personal and family maintenance has ethical implications. The division of labor at home can be a measure of how ready we are to practice the values of cooperation, communication, compassion, mutual service, and harmony in our homes.

Our attitudes about Housework can be a litmus test of our dedication to equality in the human family. The ways in which society thinks work in the home is appropriately distributed provide a model for the way male-female relationships are able to be lived out in wider society.

Housework is usually a form of work that is combined with others (though there have been those who have stretched it out to full-time.) How it is combined is a decision families have to make.

This being said, there are times when some have taken housework too seriously or disagreed in fundamental ways about how seriously it needs to be taken. The following poem tells about a woman who missed seeing Jesus because she was so busy scrubbing and dusting.

TAKING HOUSEWORK TOO SERIOUSLY

The Ballad of Befana
by Phyllis McGinley

Befana the Housewife, scrubbing her pane,
Saw three old sages ride down the lane,
Saw three gray travelers pass her door –
Gaspar, Balthazar, Melchior.
"Where journey you sirs?" she asked of them.
Balthazar answered, "To Bethlehem,
For we have news of a marvelous thing.
Born in a stable is Christ the King."

"Give him my welcome!" Then Gaspar smiled,
"Come with us, mistress, to greet the Child."

"Oh happily, happily would I fare
Were my dusting through and I'd polished the stair."

Old Melchior leaned on his saddle horn.
"Then send a gift to the small Newborn."

"Oh gladly, gladly I'd send Him one,
Were the hearthstone swept and my weaving done.
As soon as ever I've baked my bread,
I'd fetch Him a pillow for His head,
And a coverlet too," Befana said.
"When the rooms are aired and the linen dry,
I'll look at the Babe." But the three rode by.
She worked for a day and a night and a day.
Then, gifts in her hands, took up her way.
But she never could find where the Christ Child lay.

And still she wanders at Christmas tide,
Homeless, whose house was all her pride,
Whose heart was tardy, whose gifts were late;
Wanders, and knocks at every gate,
Crying, "Good people the bells begin!
Put off your toiling and let love in."

My heart goes out to poor Befana and I like to think that after urging others to "let love in" she found the Christ too. Befana's dilemma is real. One of the problems with housework is that it is endless and never done. One can always find something else to do. And when it was Befana's primary form of work – well who can blame her for doing it well and not wanting to leave it? Who can blame her for taking pride in her work, too often dismissed as unimportant by others?

While housework is basic to human well-being, it is a form of work, which like all other forms of work needs to be done with an eye to balance. Other work is indeed important and time consuming, whether it be parenting children, caring for infirm elders, making money, or volunteering in community. In all work, we need to come to terms with when enough is enough . . . or too much is too much. We ask ourselves how this work serves life itself and our deepest values.

As we noted in the ideal image, society has promoted the idea that a woman's worth can be measured by the cleanliness and beauty of her home. The effects of cultural stereotyping are still with us so that women often have more of an investment in the aesthetics of the home than men and a harder time setting limits on that work.

Adults in a household can and often do have different personal housekeeping standards and ideas about how clean is clean. Partners can disagree on what matters most: some like a home neat and picked up and others want it clean in the corners and under the beds but don't mind clutter. Families are trying to strike a balance between compulsively spotless and reasonably clean.

Theoretically, mothers once had systems for cleaning and times of year when it was all done thoroughly. I used to sing as a child: "Monday, wash day, Tuesday, ironing, Wednesday" . . . I have forgotten how it goes! My life, our lives are not like that anymore.

In an interdependent family style, there may not be anyone at the heart of family comings and goings anymore who is solely responsible for housework. Family life is a team effort. Everyone is in motion. The shift from mother centered and father dominated homes to more open and flexible ones can be disorienting. It can also be satisfying and contribute to family bonding and cooperation.

Standards vary. How beautiful is a home to be, how wrinkle free must clothes be, how elaborate should meals be, how dust free tables? We are leaving behind the notion that cleanliness and godliness go hand-in-hand. At the same time, we are becoming more conscious of the relationship between cleanliness and health, food and good nutrition, and aesthetics and happiness.

A family is a small business with a building to maintain, personnel to administer, finances to manage, services to render, commerce to support. Through the work we do at home we run this enterprise. It is no minor system. The sum of these small businesses is one of the major markets for big business. In all of our comings and goings, we have to maintain our "small businesses" so that the social order can thrive. We are entrepreneurs and consumers.

Housework is here to stay. In order to more easily organize housework, make it accessible to all family members, and discuss it rationally, I have divided housework into three kinds of tasks: Personal caretaking, caring for shared space and activities, and domestic arts.

THE TASKS OF PERSONAL MAINTENANCE

Personal maintenance, a good measure of housework, is the work of keeping one's self clean, clothed, and one's personal things and environment ordered. The work of personal maintenance includes everything that has to do with an individual's private care: brushing teeth, washing, dressing, snacking, and along with these things, cleaning up bathtubs and sinks, picking up dishes, organizing belongings, washing, drying, sorting, putting away clothes, the list goes on. All of this is part of personal care and can be undertaken by individuals as they are able. We should not have to do these things for others unless they are too young, too old, too sick or disabled to do them themselves.

Making sure that every human being is responsible for their own personal maintenance doesn't appear difficult on the surface of it. But who wouldn't want someone to do most of these personal chores for us if we could get away with it? Yet, being so entitled is bound to have a subtle, perhaps not so subtle, effect on life together as a family.

Children who learn to take care of themselves and their own environment, with adults setting an example, learn a pattern of responsible egalitarian living that is likely to carry over into the wider community. They are not only learning dependability, they are learning to value others. None of the simple tasks of personal maintenance require skilled labor. They take time, organization and a willingness to do them and support for the doing.

It is difficult for people to learn mutual respect in households where females serve males' and children's very personal needs on a routine and daily basis. A friend remembers very vividly and with anger how she as the one girl in a household with four brothers had to wait on them when she was growing up. She felt used and a second-class person in her own home.

In theology, one of the images we refer to when speaking of God's present and coming Order is "The Household of God." For those of us for whom this imagery has meaning, we can see that when we teach every member of a household to be responsible for their own personal maintenance, we are defining one very basic aspect of the "Household of God": no one is entitled to be waited on by sheer virtue of gender. Caring for one's self is simply a part of living and respecting oneself and others.

WORK AROUND A FAMILY'S COMMON LIFE

Not all housework is an extension of personal maintenance. Some housework has to do with a family's common life. There are areas of the house that are used corporately. There are meals eaten in common. There are rooms that are available for everyone's use. There are budgets that support the whole family, transportation that is shared, lawns or porches, or stoops, that all enjoy, walks that everyone uses, and the list goes on.

Some of the common work of family life requires skilled labor, other work is fairly routine requiring little skill. Many families I know decide who does what by figuring out who wants to do what, who is available when a particular chore needs to be done, and who is best fit to do it. Today almost all family housework is negotiable and most family members are learning one new skill or another with some work clearly needing to fall to adults.

Family life may have seemed easier when couples assumed that everything inside of the house was women's work and men's work was everything outside. When families need to decide who will do what, it becomes clear that sharing work really makes it easier and more interesting. People need to talk to one another, plan together, and help each other out.

Adults will need to select and buy food and they can invite the input of children, helping them learn about nutrition and health. Adults will be in charge of the family budget but children can engage in general discussions about money that will prepare them for their later handling of finances and living within a budget.

The family can work out the use of common space together. How can we plan to eat meals together and who will prepare them? When will we watch television and how much? When will homework be done and where? When will adults have time for each other? Organizing home space for family use and personal comfort is everyone's business.

In our family, when our sons were old enough to pitch in, we all rotated responsibility for cooking. I loved being surprised by some of the creative meals they came up with, like chicken cooked in coke. It worked.

The advantages to sharing a family's common life are real. Every family member has an investment in the home. Love includes physically caring for one another. Family members learn to work together and communicate. The distasteful tasks can be spread around and the enjoyable ones shared. And what some people hate doing, others may actually enjoy. If a family is lucky and everyone cooperates, it can plan work so that people can do the things they like doing and do best or at least, the work they dislike least and can do reasonably well.

Judy, a single mom and suburban math teacher, told us that her children share in the housework. She felt that this was an important part of their moral education.

"They all make up their beds. They all keep their rooms clean. They can cook for themselves. I mean, I'm not saying they cook big meals, but they know how to make eggs and soup. I think they can provide for themselves quite adequately. They have been taught that they should clean up when they're done."

The administration of shared housework is an organizational challenge. Even when parents strive toward the development of a democratic life style in the home, they retain and need authority as heads of the household to enable structure, to set limits, to establish agendas, to set a moral tone, and to ensure time for fun and play. But eliciting cooperation in housework is not easy. Everyone has other important things to do, including children with school and outside activities.

In public people are fined for trashing the environment. We can't fine family members in the home for trashing the place. It is probably better to encourage good will, cooperative spirits, in a positive atmosphere to make it all work. When we think about housework, we can think, "everyone's work." "Women's work" won't cut it anymore . . . neither will "Nobody's work."

A good meal, an anesthetically pleasing environment, feels good. It is a source of sensual pleasure and inner peace. It is worth some time and effort and organization.

THE ART PART OF DOMESTIC WORK

Housework can be drudgery. It can also be meditative, playful, or artful work.

Kathleen Norris, in *The Cloister Walk*, described the satisfaction Benedictines derive from simple community chores that are part of everyday ritual and life. Maybe housework could be a little like that for family members. Good, solid, centering, even meditative ritual.

One of the beautiful and peaceful things about life in the monastery is the way in which simple things take on new meaning when they are done mindfully in community.

Some people may find housework relaxing, focusing on it in the present and allowing it to take away the other stresses of life as long as it is not surrounded by family chaos and confusion. In some

Buddhist communities as in Christian monastic settings, people who hold everything in common see housework as a spiritual discipline. It is good physical labor shared by all.

We can recover some of the ritual potential in housework and retain some of its art. Once housework is seen as everyone's or anyone's work, we can begin to recover some of its value in bringing us together in shared space, shared sacred space.

Kathryn Allen Rabuzzi, in *The Sacred and the Feminine: Toward a Theology of Housework*, has also called this "sacred work" because the home is a place of ultimate concern.

> " . . . to be centered is to be in the middle of whatever exists. It is to be a self within a world. But as existential analytic theory suggests, the worlds in which we all stand are not single, but multiple. There is Umwelt, the environment generally thought of as the natural world, Mitwelt, the world of fellow humans, generally called community, and Eigenwelt, the world of relationship to oneself, which presupposes self-awareness. The latter two worlds are unique to humans, but Umwelt is present to all sentient beings. To center yourself in the sense that Home allows is specifically to center yourself within the Eigenwelt: to be at home with yourself. This ability to be at home with yourself relates directly to the fact that home, as opposed to a merely profane house, functions as a symbol of both salvation and damnation, making it above all a symbol of ultimate concern."

Rabuzzi sees the home as the "Eigenwelt," the world of relationship to oneself. It is also the Mitwelt, the world of being in relationship with others. She sees the place where we are in relationship to ourselves and to significant others as central to our well being, a place as she says of "ultimate concern."

Rabuzzi sees the home as sacred space and therefore caring for it as a spiritual discipline. She argues for taking housework beyond subsistence work to meaningful work. This may seem impossible to people trying to balance four jobs at once, but it may also suggest a way to ground our daily living in meaning.

As we share in the work of caring for a home and tend to the work of caring for ourselves, maybe we can begin to find simple pleasure in these basic tasks we do. In our increasingly technological world, those tasks connect us to the physical, to the essential, to the ordinary aspects of life in a complex impersonal world.

Walking down the path to my sister's home is always such a joy. She has planted flowers of every hue, shape, size and fragrance there. Butterflies enjoy the blossoms. And I find a few moments of beauty, pleasure and solace there. It never ceases to amaze me that she has grown many of them from seeds and planted them with her own hands.

There are ways in which housework is an open door, a beginning place for domestic arts. Cooking can be creative; making bread, jelly, cookies, a favorite soup or salad, a good meal. One of our co-grandparents is a great baker. Decorating a home can be a way to create one's own art space. Mother did beautiful decoupage and embroidery which I treasure. My sister-in-law crochets and works in wood, my brother-in-law makes hope chests and handcrafted toys. One of our doctors loves the rose garden he has planted and has created a "Healing Garden" at the hospital with which he is affiliated. These family members and friends are not alone. Our kitchen table was made by our son when he was in Junior High School. Out of home workrooms and fertile imaginations come rugs, quilts, holiday decorations.

I wonder if future generations will continue this form of human fulfillment and cultural expression. These art forms can be therapeutic for the creator and nurturing for the appreciator.

The Rev. Babby Cameron, after returning from a trip which revolved around providing wool for Bosnian women, reported that Bosnian women, having lived through unimaginable terrors and now living in refugee camps, found that they could finally talk with one another about the horror they had witnessed as they sat around in knitting circles, their fingers flying, their eyes downcast, as they brought some of their "homework" into the group.

Some work related to domestic art is fulfilling and healing. Some of the work women and men have done at home may be on the endangered list, home cooking, sewing and knitting, woodworking, gardening. But we may be experiencing a reawakening and reclaiming of this work.

We can imagine God still creating and sustaining the world, participating with creation in work both great and ordinary, we can imagine God in the image of Housekeeper. With God we can care for the world as household, creating beauty and comfort in our daily sanctuaries, our homes. This hymn is about Washerwoman God. It could be about Washerman God. (The computer recognized Washerwoman as a word but not Washerman.)

THE DIVINE HOUSEKEEPER

The Divine Housekeeper
(Martha Ann Kirk, 1985)

Washer woman God, we know you in the waters,
Washer woman God, splashing, laughing free!
If you didn't clean the mess, where would we be?
Scrubbing, working, sweating God,
Cleansing you and me.
Make our hearts as bright as snow,
Wash us through and through.
Washer woman, let us be like you.

Housework is honest work that we can all do. We can imagine it as God's own Work, God as a Washer Woman . . . or Man.

In Jesus' day, it was a custom to have one's feet washed by another after a day's travel or hard work. One day, Jesus went to the disciples and began to wash their feet. Peter was flustered and protested. How can my teacher wash my feet?

Jesus washing Peter's feet disturbed Peter's hierarchy of power. Menial tasks were not performed by those in power! Jesus told Peter in no uncertain terms that he was setting an example for all of them to follow. If their teacher could wash Peter's feet, they could wash one another's feet. They could serve one another, performing this menial task in love. Figuratively speaking, washing each other's feet can be a spiritual experience.

Every time a family shares the ordinary tasks of keeping a home clean, preparing meals, doing laundry, they are sharing symbolically in a foot-washing ritual of equality. In God's economy everyone is equal.

Mutuality is a key to love, to doing justice and to pursuing peace. It has to be learned in our homes. Christian ethics calls us both to value housework because it is part of caring for and being stewards of creation, and to see this work as part of our mutual service to one another.

Caring for our homes is precursor to caring for the whole environment – which we must care for if we are to survive. Learning to live in mutual respect at home is part of creating a just society without which there is no peace.

The way we relate to one another in the home forms the basis for our understanding of social relationships outside of the home. Susan Okin, writing in *Justice, Gender and the Family*, says, speaking of traditional family life, . . . "it is not conducive to the rearing of citizens with a strong sense of justice. In spite of all the rhetoric about equality between the sexes, the traditional or quasi traditional division of family labor still prevails."

The patriarchal family keeps patriarchal society in business and the conservative politicians know it. What happens in the family has repercussions beyond the home.

HOUSEHOLDS DOING HOUSEWORK IN THE FUTURE

Housework is not complicated, it is just very daily. Women and men and children sharing this work is the way of the future. This constitutes a challenge to traditional family patterns and mind sets.

Change takes real energy and will. It requires the learning of new skills and the development of new patterns. It requires the reeducation of our psyches and beliefs. In some homes, the issue of who does the house work continues to constitute a power struggle. In other homes, who does what is more a matter of habit than anything else. For still others, housework is a bother and finding time for it is of no value. For all of us, finding new ways to get the basic work of living done can take some of the stress out of life.

Jesus said, "the least of you shall be the greatest." The least of the work that all of us do may, in the last analysis, be supremely important to our social and spiritual well being. Our homes are the learning ground for relationships, for developing respect for one another and for our environment. They can be our havens. We may never love housework, but we may learn to take it in stride and value it.

Just as our bodies are our sanctuaries, our homes are part of sacred space. Caring for them can bring fulfillment and satisfaction. Those of us who have places to live that we can call home are very fortunate. And homes lead to housework. It takes a household to do the housework. God's household is an imagined place of equality, comfort, and peace. Who can presume to care about the earth and our environment without caring about and being invested in the places we call home?

CHAPTER 4

PAID WORK

Life has its beginning and end
But it's the in-between that matters
Process is vital
Creation is still in the making

PAID WORK IS the second kind of work that we undertake in life. Our first forays into the world of paid work usually begin when we are adolescents, earning pocket money, supporting our education, and sometimes contributing to the family's income as we prepare for our life as adults when we have to earn money to survive.

I remember my first job. It was summer and our family was in Ocean City, New Jersey. I packed salt water taffy for a penny a box and felt very proud about earning money.

Eric Erickson identified "Industry," in *Childhood and Society*, as the fourth stage of human development.

" . . . this is a socially most decisive stage: since industry involves doing things with and beside others, a first sense of division of labor and of differential opportunity, that is a sense of the technological ethos of culture, develops at this time." " . . . before the child, already a rudimentary parent, can become a biological parent, he (sic) must begin to be a worker and potential provider."

A significant part of our human development includes our learning to labor in the world. Our physical survival is connected to our right and responsibility to earn money or its equivalent or to be supported by someone who does.

Our paid work gives us a sense of independence in an interdependent world, a connection with colleagues, an opportunity to participate in the public realm, and a way to relate to those social systems and networks that keep the wheels of our political, economic, and cultural systems turning.

Employment contributes to our sense of identity and self worth in multiple ways. Through it we can hone our abilities and if we are lucky, find a sense of purpose and meaning in our employment.

Through our corporate labors we keep commerce, politics, education, science, construction, medicine, law, religion, art, education, and the media, all going.

Stephan Cardinal Wyszynski, writing in *All You Who Labor*, says:

"Our mind, will, feeling, and physical strength share in work." And then, "Of course, the kind of work we do determines the participation our mind, feeling, or physical powers have in it. But there is no work from which they can be fully separated."

There was a time when paid work was seen as men's responsibility, right, and burden – with some exceptions. Unmarried women (known as "spinsters," or "old maids") could work alongside men. Single mothers had to work to keep themselves and their children afloat. Poor married women were employed alongside of their husbands so the family could survive. When middle class married women worked outside of the home they were seen as earning "pin money," not being bread winners.

Today, men and women are in the workforce in almost equal numbers, women and men of all socio-economic groups and ethnic origins. This is a tremendous shift away from the old paradigm and the Ideal Good Worker.

THE IDEAL WORKER

The Ideal Worker is a man. As head of his household he is responsible for the financial support of his family, and is expected to take his place in the world outside of the home as their protector. He is dependent on his wife to make a home and care for their children. He deserves to be fully appreciated and supported in his job.

The job held by the Good Worker, or the income he derives from it, determines the family's status in society. They benefit from his accomplishments and suffer from his failures or misfortunes. Their devotion and loyalty to him reflect well on him. Any lack of support on their part will, it is presumed, interfere with his achievements and undermine him.

He is a loyal employee or faithful practitioner of his trade. Society takes it for granted that a man's work can be hard, demanding, time consuming, and sometimes dangerous. The social milieu in which it takes place is competitive and sometimes cut-throat. If he is in an institutional setting, he, at the same time, functions within an established hierarchy as a team player.

The Good Worker's maleness enables him to negotiate the harsh realities of the world by being strong and being a team player. Work is much like sports in the values it promotes: respect for authority, fighting to win, taking whatever lumps come, knowing the rules of the game, showing team loyalty, giving one's all. It's all part of the game.

As a member of a team, the Worker can accomplish bigger things than he could ever accomplish alone. There are clear rewards for playing within the system and penalties for taking it on.

The Good Worker is protector of his own family through his worldliness and strength. He is responsible for guarding and keeping those who depend on him for survival. If that means taking risks, even risks that could lead to the loss of his life, he must take them. That is part of his duty. He must soldier on.

The Good Worker must be at home with violence and accept it as the "way of the world." He cannot be "soft" or "naïve" about reality.

The Good Worker is an extension of a God of power who provides for creation. God gives the Good Provider his life responsibilities and failing at them constitutes moral failure. Keeping the trust he is given aligns him solidly with Divine power. Industriousness in the Worker is essential to Godliness.

Within this ideal lies an ethic that says man has value and an identity because he works, and through this work, he is given dominion over all creation. Man knows who he is by what he does for a living. Without *doing* there is the danger of slipping into *non-being*.

A CHANGING IDEAL

This image like all ideal images is an exaggeration. Nonetheless, it describes many aspects of men's lives as they existed in previous generations and it identifies pressures men still face.

My own father was a hard worker and a good provider. He worked diligently, was successful, and felt at home in the world. Because of him, I felt secure and confident in my environment. I loved having someone pay my way and look out for me, and having a mother and grandmother who took care of all our needs at home. I understand the appeal of the ideal.

We have those men and women who lived into much of the "ideal" to thank for keeping society running and putting bread on our tables. They were the miners who brought coal from the bowels of the earth, the doctors who cared for us when we were sick, the people in factories who manufactured things and the farmers who produced food, the police and firemen who protected us, the teachers who taught us, the clergy who spoke with us of faith, the technicians who fixed things, those who went to war.

These workers were a mixed group. Some of them loved what they were doing, others hated their work and many were just doing their job. Most workers were husbands and fathers as well as earners.

We celebrate and give thanks for the work done by so many before us, and as we do, we recognize some of the ways that life was hard as well as satisfying for them. We can appreciate the past without accepting the "ideals" and paradigms which set its parameters even though they are so familiar.

Today, we know that not all employed people and heads of household are men. In fact, in the past they were not all men – although some still think that is the way life "should" be. Even mothers who are employed and men who care for children can continue to believe in the stereotypes when their own lives veer from them.

Joan was an outstanding educator. Her husband, Paul, worked for the transit authority. They both enjoyed their work and were happy in their marriage. They raised a child together. And yet, whenever women and men's life roles were discussed, they held fast to the idea that women ought not to work for pay. That was men's responsibility. They lived outside of the ideal but continued to believe in it.

Another man was an "ideal worker" and so threatened by the very idea of his wife working that he assured us that the day his wife went to work, he would quit, lie down on the sofa, and never get up. He lived and believed in the ideal.

On the other hand, my friend and colleague, Charles, neither lived the ideal nor believed in it. He and his wife were both bread winners and believed that that was the direction in which society was moving. They recognized the need for economic parity between the sexes and believed the ideal was hard on both women and men.

Then there have always been those who, for whatever reason, were never in a position to participate in the "ideal," or were excluded from it for periods of time, because of poor health, racial, gender, or age discrimination, economic challenges or underemployment and unemployment.

The American dream, with husband as breadwinner and wife as homemaker, has been hard to give up and equally hard to live up to. Even in modern times it can seem somewhat seductive because of its strong religious roots, promise of a secure economic base and social status, and what seem to be strong family values and the implementing of men's and women's true nature.

The ideal is connected to the Protestant work ethic and has its equivalent in other religious systems and in secular myth. Speaking of that ethic, the Rev. Dr. Norman Faramelli has this to say:

> "That ethic, despite its many values, has exacted a terrible cost. One major cost was that it has resulted in an overemphasis on the value of work in the life of the individual and society. In the worst form of the Protestant Work ethic, what we do on our jobs becomes close to identifying who we are as human beings. Theologically, if that view is asserted, we fail to see that we are children of God and that our worth in the eyes of God is independent of what we do on the job."

In today's society we are trying to define and affirm employment on our own terms. We can affirm the centrality of employment in our lives while being very clear about the ways in which we intentionally move from the ideal to define our own places in the marketplace and our own being apart from it.

One aspect of the ideal worker that has changed dramatically is the assumption that the Ideal Worker had a wife at home. Most employees simply don't have a spouse at home during most of their working lives. Actually, having a wife at home had its down side. It allowed the marketplace great latitude in establishing hours, setting travel schedules, and moving employees around. The worker was freed from having to pay attention to daily maintenance tasks at home and the care of children. He was also deprived of many of the satisfactions of being close to his children. Since half of the workforce is composed of women today, most of whom are wives and parents, basic assumptions about the family life of workers need to change.

This is just one fundamental change. There are others. Men have been employed as a class far longer than women and have been the ones who were expected to live up to the image of the Ideal Worker and who now have an opportunity to be liberated from him.

IDENTITY AND EMPLOYMENT

Our society has traditionally placed a high value on the man who is dedicated to his paid work and whose identity is tied up with being a breadwinner. We are afraid along with him that if he loses his job, he will lose himself. Even in our post-feminist world, men still feel a great burden for the economic support of families and society continues to place that burden on them.

James Dittes writes these words in his book, *When Work Goes Sour*:

> "This is also the terrible secret of men; behind the swagger, behind the one-sided love affair with work, behind the reliance on work and working to provide, behind the posturing that our work proves us strong, there is that well-kept, not so well-kept, secret that men have turned to their work out of fear that without it they are nothing. The liberation from the enslaving pact with the oppressor, whoever and whatever the oppressor, is in the conversion from the feeling of emptiness and nothingness . . . . Liberation is in the much more radical conversion to feeling no longer needy, no longer hungry for the fix – the conversion to feeling sturdy, resourced, upright, empowered from within and not from outside, not from being without, not from any beings without."

Men have a right to embrace paid work fully and find satisfaction in it without giving up their personal power or losing a sense of personal power when unemployed or doing other kinds of work. Personal power comes from within as Dittes suggests and withstands the driving pressures for approval based on some ideal image.

Men deserve social and familial support in asserting their identity outside of employment and worth within it. Men need liberation from those forces within employment that are harmful to their health and their relationships, and, in their opinion, potentially hazardous to the common good.

There is another dimension to employment and identity, our institutional and communal connections. Because employment connects us with activities, networks, vocations that give us an institutional identity as well as a livelihood, the loss of those connections, whatever the reason, can leave us feeling stranded, and stripped of an important part of our identity as well as financially crushed.

When I left my job at Harvard Divinity School at the end of my five year contract, we lost the second mortgage on our home as well as my salary. I also lost the advantages and prestige of being identified with a powerful institution and all of the benefits that accords. I was not only unemployed, I was deinstitutionalized. I had to reaffirm my identity as a valuable person outside of my association with Harvard.

A family in our church moved to the Boston area because the wife had been hired in a high level position in a local high tech firm. Her husband left a good job to move with her. Finding new employment was not easy for him. He had willingly left his job to move with her. As the months passed by without his finding work, he felt a deep anxiety that nothing seemed able to relieve. He had lost connections to work he loved. When he eventually found a job, he experienced a return of his equilibrium. In the whole process, he had discovered some strengths in himself that he didn't know he had. Looking back on the experience, he found that while employment had a unique place in his life, he has worth apart from it. That was liberating.

One of things we discovered in our early study of employed mothers was that they had different levels of investment in their paid work. Personality types, family relationships, and economic needs all fed into their identificaton with paid work. For some women, work for pay was just a job. For others work for pay was a career. Since that first study, I have noticed that men also have different levels of investment in paid work.

What makes paid work a job or a career is a person's desire to advance in their work, to take work home in their head with them. Some people simply find their work more fulfilling than others do. Career-oriented people need to express themselves through their work and are willing to make sacrifices in other areas of life in order to succeed.

Whether people see their work as a job or career does not seem to depend on the kind of work they do. An office administrator was very career oriented, wanting more responsibility in her job, taking courses at night to advance in her position. On the other hand, a medical doctor who married late in life, willingly gave up her employment when she married. Then there is Terry Francona, manager of the Boston Red Sox, who was asked in a television interview how he combines his family relationships with his work. "With great difficulty," he replied. Sometimes our employment itself determines how closely identified with it we have to be.

In a dialogue on Masculinity and Fatherhood between two pioneers on the subject, Joseph Pleck says, "When I read the brief biographies of the men lost on 9/11, I'm struck that their family lives define them as much as or more than their work."

People find their identity through employment in different ways and to different degrees. For each person, paid work takes on meaning that is specific to who they are and their circumstances.

TIME

One of the early achievements of labor unions was the establishment of the forty hour week for hourly workers. No such boundaries were set for salaried employees. In fact, the unspoken assumption was that the more hours one worked, the more committed and effective one was. The Ideal Worker was a hard worker and this was demonstrated by time put in.

Modern workers can be as committed to their jobs and careers as the "Ideal Worker" was supposed to be, without buying into the concept that effectiveness and dedication can be measured by hours worked. Too many people who have developed this concept have allowed work to take over their lives.

Diane Faisal, in *Working Ourselves to Death*, identifies our society as one in danger of making ourselves sick with work. She sees us as a workaholic society and names workaholism as a social disease that, rather than improving work performance, hinders it.

> "Workaholism is a compulsion, a disease. No amount of willpower will prevent the classic alcoholic from reaching for a drink; no amount of good resolution will stop the workaholic. Of course, what compounds the problem for the workaholic is a social structure that rewards work addiction. No wonder our radio call-ins are confused. They have internal signals telling them that something is wrong with the way they are working, but externally our society is giving them a series of positive myths about workaholism. It is through these myths that society establishes work addiction as the norm and numbs us to the disastrous effects of the disease."

Women, like men, can fall into the overworking trap, but the trap is really laid for men. There is nothing ideal about working obsessively. One of the hopeful changes in the ideal is in men's wanting to work reasonable hours, leaving time for other kinds of work and leisure. Time in the new economy is a valued commodity. Women's sharing the economic burden of supporting the family with men helps bring more balance into life. Basic changes in workplace expectations are on the horizon.

Steven and Rebecca, after much discussion and soul searching, decided to share the work of bread winning and parenting. Steve was a computer programmer and quickly got a job at a high salary. Rebecca got a job as a childcare worker. They have two children, four year old Paul and five year old John. Steve's company expected him to work long hours. While he tried to work a typical forty hour week, he rarely could. He wasn't home as much as either he or Rebecca would have liked. As a consequence, she ended up doing more of the housework and parenting than he did, but he was wanting to do more and really enjoyed parenting. They both felt that their work outside of the home contributed to their children's understanding of life. And sharing work responsibilities brought them closer together even though they often felt stretched for time. They were reaching for a new life style.

Their current life style worked even though it was not perfect. And they vowed that over time they would adjust the amount of work they each did at home and on the job. Paul continued to ask for what he and his family needed and eventually he was able to work more reasonable hours and have more family time.

Paul felt secure enough in his job that he did not worry about losing it. For many, however, in an unstable economy, that fear is real. Unemployment, which is usually first and foremost a financial problem, can also bring with it social and emotional stress.

Some workers struggle at the other extreme of too little work. Employment can be hard to find. Roy lost his job as a janitor when his company downsized. Without a formal education, he was limited in the work available to him. His family of four children went on welfare in order to survive. At one point, he was offered a position as an aide in a nursing home at a salary that paid less than what they were getting on welfare and on which his family could not survive. They were squeaking by on welfare. He desperately wanted to work but he had to say no to that job. There was great social pressure on him to take the job but if he did, his family would starve. If welfare had been willing to supplement his income at the nursing home or the nursing home could match his income from welfare then Rob could have had the satisfaction of the employment he longed for, and some independence. The emotional bind this put him in was excruciating

In another family, the wife's unemployment had serious economic consequences. It meant the loss of the family's home. While the family was able to rent another home based on the husband's salary alone, the experience left scars. They had worked hard to buy a home and many dreams were tied up with that place. Add to their sense of loss, Jill's losing a job she enjoyed.

Time put in was not a factor in these people losing their jobs. Yet the ideal suggested that if men were unemployed it was because of some failing on their part. Most unemployment comes not because a person is not working hard enough or putting in enough time, but because work has dried up, a job is outsourced, internal politics are at work, a company has to reorganize or is going out of business, or family circumstances require a focus on another form of work, such as care-taking.

The ideal also suggested that if a man worked hard enough he could support his family on his income. However, there have always been and still are those among us who work full time and do not make a living wage.

LIVING WAGES

In the Ideal image, if a worker worked full time, he could sustain his family on his income, even if at a very basic level. In today's world, this is a false assumption. It is possible for a man or woman to work full time and not earn a living wage, as we saw in the case of Roy in the previous section. When some of us pray, "Give us this day our daily bread," we are not looking for handouts. We are willing to work for what we need.

Continuing to raise the minimum wage, especially for those of an age to support themselves financially, is important to solving this issue but it is not enough. And all of us need to concern ourselves with the working poor. The federal government's minimum wage was set at

$6.25 until in July 2009 it is $7.25. It is impossible to support a family on $14,500 a year almost anywhere in the United States.

Kate Lorenz of Career Builder lists the 25 lowest paying jobs in America. These all come in under $18,500 for full time work. Among the jobs listed are those related to the care of children and elders, those that provide protection for recreational activities, farm workers, food preparers, and retailers. Anyone who goes into these fields is providing services for society at an economic cost to themselves.

Some of the work that is poorly paid is what we have come to call "unskilled labor." One way we can address the issue of the working poor is by job training, and educational advancement. However, even when we have done that, some people will need to or choose to work as so-called "unskilled laborers." They deserve to live on what they earn.

Since women make up a disproportionate number of the working poor, correcting inequities in salaries between women and men can be of some help.

Barbara Einrich and Karen Stallard cite women's segregation in the world of work as the second greatest cause of poverty among women. They say, "women's work not only pays less than men's but is less inflation proof. The Bureau of Labor Statistics reports dramatic decline in real earnings for the sectors of the work force in which women are concentrated such as services and clerical work."

Exacerbating the problem is the high cost of health care and the fact that many in low paying positions go without health care of any kind. Those workers in low paying jobs who get benefits can survive much more easily than those without any. And those parents with adequate vacation time have the benefit of not having to negotiate summers for their children. However, most workers in low paying jobs do not have good benefits or much vacation time.

I was amazed to learn that someone employed full-time, initially had only one week of paid vacation a year. This will increase over time. But if a worker is a parent, this jeopardizes not only an individual's well being, but the life of the family.

Today, the middle class is feeling economic stresses even when they are earning living wages, often with two family members working full time. Given the economic obligations of most middle class families, they are one or two paychecks away from poverty themselves. The economics of the workplace have changed. In *"The Two Income Trap,"* we find these words:

> "The collective pressures on the family – the rising cost of educating their children, the growing insurance payments and medical bills, the rising risks of layoffs and plant closures, and the unscrupulous tactics of an unrestrained credit industry – are pushing families to the breaking point. America's middle class is strong, but its strength is not unlimited."

Add to the pressures on modern families the cost of gas, the declining housing market, credit card fees, and the rising cost of food. The time has come for the workforce to assert itself, men and women acting together, to solve some justice issues as marketplace, homeplace, and life style meet.

The usurious practices of credit card companies and mortgage companies need to be reined in even as Americans adjust their spending to match their budget. As middle America tightens its belt, it has a right to expect salaries at the top to be less exorbitant, salaries at the low end to be more fair, and benefits to be more secure for everyone.

At the high end of the earning scale are those who make millions of dollars a year in addition to stock options. The yawning gap is indefensible. As we pay attention to paid work in our society we can pressure institutions to correct for disparity. Some shareholders have already begun to take action to address the issue of excessive salaries at the top. The redistribution of unethically high salaries is necessary to prevent the lay-off of hourly workers and middle management.

Anyone who works for pay is not only serving their own or a given institution's interests but the interest of the entire community in which they ply their trade. The fair wages issue has to do with how much is too little and how much is too much. It also has to do with how we treat those who find themselves unemployed.

Clearly, when unemployment occurs we need safety nets: extended employment benefits, extensions on home mortgages, job retraining, support, programs to keep families afloat until they can sustain themselves again.

Ellen Goodman in an op-ed piece in the Boston Globe makes note of the fact that women have closed another gap between themselves and men. Men and women are now unemployed in equal numbers. (These figures are constantly changing. However, the gap does not shift much.)

Connected with the issue of earnings is another issue, the contrast in wages between those in the service sector of society and those in the financial and business sector.

COMPENSATING THE SERVICE SECTOR

Implicit in the Ideal is the notion that when women are employed, they are suited for certain kinds of work. That work best suited to women requires "feminine" traits and work more suited to men "masculine" traits. Those doing jobs requiring so-called male characteristics received higher salaries than those engaged in work requiring so-called feminine characteristics. Now men and women are employed in both "masculine" and "feminine" sectors.

Several years ago, at a meeting of a community development organization in our area, the Board was discussing salary discrepancies between staff members. Those who worked on housing development were making more money than those who worked with the meals program. The discrepancy was explained. The housing program creates income for the corporation. Those working in that arena have to deal with banks and politicians, the power brokers of the community. They need to be paid well to work and be respected in that venue.

The meals program requires contributions of food and money to cover overhead costs. On the surface of it, it uses money, it does not make money. Those working in the meals program work with charitable and religious organizations and deal with the poor. While they may save society money by helping to feed people and enable them to participate in society, they do not produce wealth. The differences in staff salaries were justified on these bases.

In the ideal image, those who create wealth are rewarded more highly than those who provide services in the social sector. By recognizing the monetary value of education and service work we can contribute to a reconceptualization of what constitutes appropriate compensation for various kinds of work in our society.

Quantifying the value different kinds of work have in the whole economic scheme of things is not easy. We can begin by measuring the money that society saves and the resources that society gains by those who are educators, those who help maintain order, and those who bring relief to the suffering. These monetary gains compare favorably with the value to society of the production and creation of wealth.

Tufts University has found a creative way to begin to address this issue. They have a program that encourages graduating seniors to choose careers in the service sector by adjusting their undergraduate loans to support and enable this choice.

By providing nurturing, educational, medical, sales, and social services for people we can avoid more costly care and disasters down the road, in addition to contributing to human well being.

Valuing both the so-called "masculine" world of technology, production and economics and the so-called "feminine" world of human services, education, and art is essential to our nation's future interests. Our capitalistic know-how has far outstripped our human know-how and moral development. We have not yet fully used our creative energy to this end.

We could become an underdeveloped nation by not addressing human development as seriously as we address economic development.

As Americans, we now have men and women employed in equal numbers. It is time to value so-called "feminine" and "masculine" endeavors equally as we enter a time of social maturity.

Another aspect of social maturity is our ability to create a genuinely humane work environment.

IT DOESN'T HAVE TO BE A JUNGLE OUT THERE

The ideal worker was expected to live in a competitive, dog-eat-dog environment when necessary. Of course, not all jobs existed in this milieu. But when they did, it was too often seen as just a part of man's world. One worker described feeling as if he was part of a machine and a disposable part at that.

Many men in traditionally structured work places have had to endure all kinds of stress, from competing to keep their jobs, to meeting unreasonable deadlines, to putting up with overbearing authority, to compromising their own personal values. And there can be defamation of character, power manipulations, sabotaging another's work, covering one's incompetence by blaming another. This all takes a tremendous toll on employees. We do not need to see these behaviors as normative in the workplace or in men's, and now women's, working lives.

There is for some actual physical risk-taking. As long as war or military aggression is tolerated by societies and populations, there is always the specter of young men's and some women's employment turning to soldiering in times of war.

Warren Farrell writing the *Myth of Male Power* has quite a lot to say about the effect of soldiering on men's lives:

> "The single biggest barrier to getting men to look within is that what any other group would call powerlessness, men have been taught to call power. We don't call "male-killing" sexism, we call it "glory." We don't call the one million men who were killed or maimed in one battle in World War I (the Battle of the Somme) a holocaust, we call it "serving

the country." We don't call those who selected only men to die "murderers." We call them "voters."

Farrell writes dramatically and feels strongly about these matters. Men have over time faced dangers in the workplace as well as on the battlefield that have been unknown to women. On my summer vacation this year, I looked up the record of my cousin's death in the coal mines of Pennsylvania. I was astounded to discover page after page of the names of those who had died in the mines just from the two small communities in which my father's family lived.

Some historic physical dangers of the workplace are mostly gone but new ones emerge. Men are still the employees most often in harm's way, though some women are now joining their ranks.

"Men's world" according to the patriarchal model has always had to be a more violent world than women's because that is the presumed "nature of things." As the mother of three sons, I have witnessed the ways in which the male culture of violence seemed to be always around the corner when they were growing up. Today, I look at my grandchildren. The boys are the ones playing combative video games and watching superheroes take out the opposition . . . or getting taken out themselves if they fail.

Farrell, in an agitated tone, calls men "the disposable Sex." How much of the violence children learn, especially boys, is supposed to prepare them for a rough and tumble life in the workplace and a willingness to place their lives in harm's way if necessary?

Girls can be combative too but we don't encourage them to engage in physical violence when they are growing up. I do remember playing soldier with my friends during World War II and marching around the block with imaginary rifles. But my concept of war was sanitized and totally unreal, and I knew somehow that I was never really going to be a soldier.

Women's lives were endangered in different ways in the old paradigm. Because men are breadwinners and sometimes doing dangerous work, men are fed first and women and children are fed last.

And because women are dependent on men for survival, when men died, widows were often left in poverty. Wives could be left alone to fend with the children in difficult times when men had to leave home to find paid work.

Identifying abusive workplace practices and refusing to accept them as inevitable is a first step in changing our work environment and our connections in the world. We can find alternative ways of approaching human interactions. Senator Obama, when running for President, pointed to the importance of dialogue as a first strategy for dealing with hostile nations replacing the use of force as an automatic first move. We can lay the ground work for changing our experience on the job and with that change can come a change in our entire social context.

By their nature, many work places are, in the final analysis, authoritarian systems. In the workplace, lines of authority and accountability are essential, especially in large institutions. However, within that reality there can be ethical and moral boundaries that apply to all employees, are understood corporately, and include those in positions of power.

Working in authoritarian systems without losing one's soul or one's job is a challenge worth pursuing. Authority, given a free hand, can run amok and become dehumanizing: competition can become cut-throat and ethical considerations be abandoned.

Defining ethical and moral practices that apply in employment is as critical as it is difficult. Some workplace limitations have already been enacted by law. We have regulated hours for hourly employees, safety codes, and equal employment practices: we have banned sexual harassment, and, of course, all forms of physical violence in our working context. Some harmful practices can be addressed by law and others arrived at by common consent.

Where will these values come from? As men and women work together in the marketplace, the ethical values from what has been "women's world" and "men's world" are beginning to interface and interlace. The integration of these values can be used to create a more compassionate and more effective, cooperative and creative workplace. And practices that recognize the other work responsibilities of employees, will bring about change.

There are no easy fixes for abuse or misuse of power in the workplace. Recognition and naming problems when they occur is a beginning. Having an effective, impartial grievance process is important. Calling political attention to universal issues in need of change is essential. And, of course, we all need to be aware of our own behavior in the workplace and of our expectations and attitudes. We have a right to expect humanitarian standards in our places of employment.

Studs Terkel in his classic book on work says this in the introduction:

> "This book, being about work, is, by its very nature, about violence – to the spirit as well as to the body. It is about ulcers as well as accidents, about shouting matches as well as fistfights, about nervous breakdowns as well as kicking the dog around. It is, above all (or beneath all), about daily humiliations. To survive the day is a triumph enough for the walking wounded among the great many of us."

Terkel also recognizes in the course of his writing the many ways in which some can find work fulfilling and ennobling. We can shift our working lives away from violence into the direction of fulfillment. Critical to a life-affirming work environment is our right to exercise our conscience on the job and deal overtly with unacceptable and sometimes dangerous uses of authority. Being divorced from our ethical and spiritual sensibilities when we are working does harm to the soul.

Les Kaye after training in a Zen monastery for three months returned to his job at IBM. In his book, *Zen at Work*, he talks about how his perspective has shifted:

> "Work had new contours. It no longer had a hard, 'rocky' feeling, as if I were in an endless desert of problems to

overcome and goals to attain, always in danger of stubbing my toe. Instead, work became like a garden, with new and interesting shapes, textures, and fragrances at each turn. Problems and difficulties did not go away, but my relationship with work was different. My new understanding of the meaning of success resulted in a change in priorities."

Some of the change needed is within ourselves.

EMPLOYMENT AND DEMOCRACY

The work place doesn't need to be a jungle but it can't be a democracy either. In the traditional patriarchal ideal with its polarized division of labor by gender, work places often seem to run on sets of rules and pragmatic practices developed in their own market context. Representative democracy is a political philosophy of government and not of commerce.

Global corporations can find ways to transcend the laws of nation states. The people who make it to the top, even in modern America, often function as feudal lords with their own turf to protect and their own wealth to manage. Some of our political leaders believe in unregulated economic power and a totally unhampered free market.

We now live in difficult economic times and those corporations that once fought government regulation need to be bailed out by government. In return, the government needs to explore interventions that protect both the future of businesses and the public trust.

The well being of paid workers is connected with the well being of institutions and systems that employ them. The failure of economic institutions leads to unemployment, loss of income and benefits. We can no longer afford laissez faire capitalism.

At this point in history, we need to address the complex connections between our representative democracy and the independence of the economic sector. Currently, our nation's recession (depression) is the driving force behind our bringing these worlds closer together. However, change has been simmering for some time from the ground up. There is a relationship between what is happening in families and what happens in social institutions. As we move beyond hierarchical relationships in marriage and embrace more egalitarian partnerships, we begin the long process of challenging hierarchies in the public realm.

In the public sector, the majority of men have worked under the authority of other men, often in rigid hierarchical patterns. Labor Unions developed to protect workers in what was often an inhumane context. Professional Societies were formed to advocate for the well being of their members. Many concessions were made in workplaces to improve conditions and benefit employees. But workplaces are not governments.

We cannot expect large public corporations and institutions to ever become democracies, just limited hierarchies. Functional hierarchies are necessary to get work done in complex systems with dedicated purposes. We can, however, expect these systems to be temporal and limited and fully subject to national and international law. We can expect systems of employment to operate with the long term well being of society in mind and to be fully accountable to our representative democracy.

The Ideal Worker learned to take care of his own and when necessary turn a deaf ear to the suffering of others. He functioned after all, in a no-holds-barred competitive environment. He could not worry about the whole world and could not expect the world to worry about him. Many men living outside of this narrow "ideal" did work to improve conditions in the marketplace. Today, many more men and women are conscious of a need for change in top heavy institutional structures.

Within the reality that the marketplace does not function as a democracy, there can be room for employees to have a voice in their work place, that place where they invest so much of their talents and time. While this voice will still come through labor unions, there is room for other creative avenues for self and communal expression on the part of workers, avenues that address the rights of salaried workers as well as hourly workers.

In the early seventies, The Task Force on Women of the Presbyterian Church created an association for all women employed by the church, Church Employed Women. Through that structure, church secretaries and administrators gained the right to be included in the Presbyterian Pension Plan. Women clergy advocated for the right to be considered for pastorates. Church Employed Women filled a need at a particular point in time.

Today, we need institutions of employment to be responsive to the changing nature of the workforce. Taking into account the fact that employees have parental responsibilities, we need family friendly policies. The majority balance earning money with housework and caretaking work. Vacation time, hours worked, and sick leave all need to be revisited.

Workers clearly need more job security. The political system can find ways to protect the retirement benefits of long term employees, to insure the transferability of those benefits from one company to another. Health care is a major issue of our time. It also needs to follow workers in times of job transition.

We can build economic enterprises whose strength lies in both their economic success and their ability to serve employees and society well. The time for "hands off" treatment of the employment sector is over. The fact that we live in an economically interdependent world makes this intervention even more urgent.

We live in a world in which our institutions compete with those in nations whose economies function on an entirely different scale than our own and whose treatment of employees is often below our standards. Creative minds are needed to conceive of ways to balance outsourcing and insourcing, to balance trade, and to negotiate humane standards for the treatment of all employees.

What we are searching for today is a marketplace that meets the needs of those who labor, utilizing their resources to the full, strengthening the institutions that provide goods and services. With government and commerce working together we need labor practices that foster the common good and strengthen families.

From a spiritual perspective, we need the freedom to live ethical lives on the job as well as in our private lives.

We have a right to seek out and participate in a democracy that reaches into the chambers of economic power. Protecting an employee's right to exercise conscience in the marketplace is complex but a cornerstone of a mature society.

CLAIMING OUR RIGHT OF CONSCIENCE

Do we have the right to exercise conscience in our jobs? I took a limited poll of friends and colleagues on this question and got a universal answer: "Only if we want to lose our jobs." The jobs they were talking about were as teachers, retail associates, corporate administrators, and clergy.

Everyday in the news we hear of someone in public life losing their job by breaking the law or being caught in some sexual scandal. We do not often hear about those people who lose their jobs for doing "the right thing," but it happens.

Once in awhile there is a whistle blower who is appreciated for exposing unethical behavior, like Harry Markopolos who blew the whistle on Bernard Madoff's Ponzi scheme and his multi-billion dollar bilking of clients.

When we work for pay and join society's economic enterprise and enter the world of commerce, of money and power, how much latitude do we have to follow our scruples? Can we be required to leave our religious or humanistic conscience at the door?

Every major religion has scruples when it comes to business practices. In Christianity we see that Jesus had an ethical concern for how people made their money and used their authority in the workplace. At one point in his career, he chased the money changers out of the temple for cheating people and profaning a holy place. On another occasion he challenged a rich young ruler to give up all he had and give to the poor. While this was an exaggerated request it addressed the importance of money in the ruler's life. He did not expect these actions to make him popular with those in power. He expected them to guide his followers toward reform and change.

None of the world's great religions has a tolerance for greed or usury and all speak of the need to share wealth and act as good stewards. Religions, however, have been less clear on appropriate uses of power, having all emerged in authoritarian political times.

Today we live in a democracy in the United States. Ideal workers who once were expected to do their job well and leave workplace ethical decisions to those in power, checking their own scruples at the door, need to be empowered to practice their values in the marketplace.

Women, in a patriarchal structuring of society, were expected to follow ethical codes of behavior that were different from those in the public realm. They were expected to behave morally in all aspects of their own lives and in their care taking of others. Men were allowed ethical concessions in the workplace. They were expected to be tougher, more aggressive, and more pragmatic than women. Women had to live by gentler, more compassionate, more relational morals in the home. Religious communities tended to recognize different moral expectations in men and women's work spheres and made allowances accordingly. God, after all, was the chief patriarch and used a variety of tactics, some quite violent, to achieve his will.

Today, our ethics have shifted along with our images of God. We would like the ethics of home and marketplace to meet and both serve the common good. However, we are dependent on institutions of all kinds for our bread and butter. Even raising the issue of ethics in the workplace can feel hazardous. It is a harsh reality for those whose ethics are connected with their faith, that God cannot give them what their employers can: money. So, do we dare take our conscience with us into our jobs?

Douglas Hicks, in *Religion and the Workplace*, explores the complexity and importance of recognizing faith in the marketplace. He emphasizes the fact that we can recognize the place of religion in employee's lives in the context of a pluralistic religious environment.

When we explore exercising conscience in the marketplace, we are speaking in a pluralistic context where some people are active adherents of faith and others are not. We can address the need to define the common good together even in our diversity. We have experience doing this as citizens.

Even within our complex working environments, we can as human beings be attuned to obeying just laws that are administered fairly. If we have the will to do so, in matters that fly under the radar of the law, we can reject stealing by misrepresentation, we can reject doing harm to others, either directly or indirectly, and act to protect our environment. Ultimately, following conscience means seeking common agreement on how we can live amicably and peaceably in working communities. Sometimes it means following our personal conscience on matters around which there is currently no common consensus. Then society has to wrestle with our right to follow our conscience.

We are called, through our labor, to not only serve our own needs, and those of society, but to do no harm in the process of doing our work. We are called to ethical reflection and behavior whether we are scientists, lawyers, housekeepers, teachers, builders, artists, CEOs, clergy. When we exercise our conscience, we do so for our own integrity and with the intention of serving the common good, and we have a right to legal protection or in controversial cases, the right to legal review. And there is the rub. When the law and our conscience are in conflict, we enter the realm of civil disobedience and must pay the price for our stance.

The government's recognition of conscientious objectors to war is an example of honoring religious freedom. Civil disobedience during the Civil Rights Movement was an example of the exercising of religious and conscientious freedom. People acted to change what we came to see as unjust laws by breaking those unjust laws.

Sometimes exercising conscience involves confrontation with governments or institutional systems which we see as destructive of the common good. Sometimes religious institutions are themselves responsible for gross human violations. Sometimes a whole society seems to be in collusion with evil.

In "*The Nazi Doctors,*" Robert Jay Lifton studied doctors who engaged in cruel and murderous behavior while serving in Hitler's Germany. He found that while these men could be good fathers and husbands when they were off the job, they gave themselves over to the murderous authority of the system within which they worked when on the job. Lifton called this phenomenon, "Doubling." He describes a situation in which normal people, through belief in and systematic obedience to absolute authority, participate in unspeakable systemic evil and continue to function in their private lives as ordinary men.

History has shown us that ordinary people are capable of terrible "doubling" or in less extreme ways, of living "split lives," one in the workplace and one at home, loving in the family context and committing crimes in another. Or reversing the contexts, one could act nobly in the workplace and be abusive in the family. To address this phenomenon requires our paying attention to issues of ethics, authority and behavior in the workplace and home, insisting that they be consistent and coherent. It requires giving people the freedom and protection to act on their conscience and to have this right built in to our democracy. Even today, we have many examples of people living split lives, some quite mundane and others more consequential.

A young soldier in the second Iraq War, accused of participating in the torture of prisoners, was asked on national T.V. how she could do this. She replied simply that on the job she saw no out, no alternative. She did what she had to do. She was a respectable person who was pushed beyond her boundaries in a situation in which she felt she had no alternatives.

A CEO took good care of his family but abdicated the trust of his employees by not intervening when he realized their retirement benefits were in jeopardy. Thousands lost money that was rightfully theirs. A priest betrays his parishioners by engaging in sexual misconduct and his colleagues or superiors do not report him.

As a society, we could establish judicial structures standing alongside of employment structures that protect people's right to identify misconduct when they see it, and stand up for what they believe is legally right.

Because the authority of the workplace can seem so total and compelling, because institutional loyalty is often seen as critical for advancement, and because following orders is expected, people have too often had to repress their moral sensibilities in the exercise of their on the job duties. And not all "whistle blowers," are well received or defended.

Ordinary people can commit horrendous crimes on the battlefield or in the Board Room. Salespeople with integrity at home can misrepresent the truth on the job. Workers can be divorced from the ethical implications of what they are doing. I have worked in an academic environment in which otherwise honorable people confessed that while they personally did not agree with particular corporate positions, which seemed unjust to them, they nonetheless, were going along with them as "part of a team."

Books have been written about how employees making dangerous weapons of war disassociate themselves from their end product. Living in a society which expects nothing else, anyone can go against their own better judgment and moral values in the course of their employment.

Politicians can vote to cut back on programs that feed needy children while loving and spoiling their own children. Corporate executives can execute policies which pollute the environment while being watchful and meticulous about their own children's health and doting on their grandchildren, whose lives or those of their children will ultimately be endangered by those policies.

The Ideal Worker learned to take care of his own and when necessary turn a deaf ear to the suffering of others. He could not worry about the whole world and could not expect the world to worry about him. Not all men followed this "ideal." There were those who did exercise conscience and stand up for what they considered morally right. There were those whose awareness had a global reach, who lived beyond the bounds of familial or tribal loyalty. But that was not the expected norm.

As the home and public realm come closer together, with men and women working in both venues, "splitting" or "doubling" become harder and cannot be explained away. We are moving toward integrated personalities. Institutional loyalty cannot be absolute as there are other and often higher loyalties. As paid workers we need to be able to exercise our conscience on the job in order to live as complete people. The right hand must know what the left hand is doing and take notice of it and responsibility for it.

Abuse of power in the workplace needs to be seen for the threat to society that it is and be prosecuted at the highest levels possible when it threatens the life and livelihood of others or defies principles of humane behavior.

Women who have been expected to keep humane values alive in their domain, the home, have also been expected to accept, for the family's benefit, the concessions that men have made in the marketplace. In doing so they have passively aided and abetted those concessions by living in a polarized system over which they had little control.

As we bring the workplace and the homeplace together and individuals live and work in both spheres, a philosophy in which the end justifies the means cannot be sustained. The means matter. The process matters. We are all accountable for how we get where we are going, we are responsible for "collateral" damage on our way to reaching our goals. We cannot use "following orders" as an excuse for murder and mayhem, for endangering the environment, for destroying infrastructures and creating poverty.

As long as life-giving ends are served, and society's good is promoted, we can respect hierarchies for the functional benefit they provide in achieving production and service ends. In much the same way that an orchestra follows the conductor's lead in order to make beautiful music, we can appreciate appropriate fair and accomplished authority in the workplace.

One of the valuable aspects of the old image of the "Good Provider" was his being a team player. This does not need to imply a relinquishment of self. In our Presbyterian system of governance there is a recognition of the potential for tension between dedication to the team and responsibility for one's individual integrity. Ultimately, a Presbyterian who accepts elected office in the church is called upon to exercise his or her conscience when voting and acting in halls of power as a member of the whole body.

In the final analysis, the mythic worker of the past had to show primary loyalty to the team on which he played. Sports provided a useful metaphor for our paid working lives. But life is not a game. Someone doesn't have to win and someone lose, and if they do, they don't just shake hands and walk away. People get hurt and even die. In life, we need to move toward win-win solutions and environments. The object of labor is to preserve and enhance all of life.

We have a right and responsibility, as workers in the public realm, to pursue ethical goals as well as materialistic ones in league with one another in an ethical coming-of-age.

Increasingly, the work of home and marketplace are coming together and can be seen as parts of a whole. Employees have lives outside of work that need to be honored. And "feminine" and "masculine" values and characteristics, and work styles that tend to accompany them, can be incorporated into one another and integrated. Every human being is meant to be a whole person and live as one.

EMPLOYMENT AND SEXUAL IDENTITY

Before we leave our discussion of paid work, it is important to comment on the relationship between sexuality and work.

In the traditional paradigm, men are supposed to be attracted to women as marriage partners who are willing to be dependent and home-oriented, for the purpose of establishing families. Women are supposed to be attracted to men as husbands and fathers who are strong and willing to be in charge. In the world of patriarchy men work with other men and women work in "pink-collar ghettos." Men are expected to be in charge and exercise control.

In their employment situations, men could have sexual affairs outside of marriage as long as they were discreet. The Ideal Good Worker, a man with a wife at home, was out and about and had opportunity to have sexual relationships with other women. An Ideal Mother, on the other hand, was expected to focus her sexuality (which somehow seemed diminished by motherhood) on her husband. Of course many real men were faithful to their wives and some women had affairs.

I remember that in my lifetime alone, two very popular presidents had sexual affairs with little public outcry: Franklin Delano Roosevelt and John F. Kennedy. With the advent of feminism and women's movement toward equality came laws against sexual harassment. Justice Clarence Thomas was barely approved for his position under the cloud of sexual harassment charges by Anita Hill. And Former President William Clinton was impeached for sexual indiscretions. The relationship between sexuality and work had changed at least for political figures.

As more women have entered the workforce and men and women are working together there, side-by-side and day-by-day, the dynamics are shifting. If men and women are to be equally respected co-workers in the marketplace, sexual flirtations and seductions are not appropriate. New ethical sensitivities are emerging. There is a sense that sexuality is meant to be expressed in personal intimate relationships off the job and faithfulness in marriage and other committed relationships is a renewed value.

Eugene Bianchi writes: "In monogamous intimacy trust is closely associated with fidelity. A kind of freeing hold that married persons have on one another means that they can count on a singularly devoted presence of each to the other."

Our sexuality like our spirituality is part of who we are. We can choose, however, when and where to express it. We can sublimate it and allow it to flow into our creativity. We do not need to be or turn others into sexual objects. Inappropriate sexual expression can be a form of addiction like any other.

In *Women and Gender in Islam*, Leila Ahmed quotes a woman working in the public realm who says that wearing a head scarf and dressing modestly according to her religious tradition was very freeing, because she was able to work with men without even thinking about sexuality and gender.

Having said this, we know that some people will be sexually attracted to each other at work. Some of those people will be single and eligible for relationships and others will not. Friendships will develop at work: some will be between people ready for commitment. One large company has a non-negotiable policy that if workers develop an intimate relationship at work, they must work in different departments and cultivate their relationship off company time.

If we can see the value in separating our sexuality from our employment and set out to do it well, we will be more free and focused in our places of employment and more playful and faithful in our intimate relationships.

CHAPTER 5

FAMILY WORK

Guard love carefully
Weaving thoughtfully the patterns
That will shape your days
And slip into your tomorrows.

WE NOW TURN to family work, a primary, basic form of human labor that is essential for the survival of our species and for our emotional and spiritual existence in relationship. In family settings, able adults give care to dependent family members and oversee the care given to them by others. Dependent family members can be children, parents with medical issues, or other relatives with special needs.

Love connects us to one another in the intimate bonds particular to family life. Because of those intimate bonds, family work also has unique challenges. Anyone who has done caretaking work knows that it requires skill and the wisdom of Solomon. In the past, this was seen as women's work. And since men's primary role in the family was as bread winner and protector, life in the market place was structured on the assumption that those men who worked for pay should not have to be distracted by the tasks of caring for others.

As we have moved toward a time when all four forms of work are being done by women and men in a variety of life style patterns, pragmatic reality opens the door for us to rethink old assumptions. Some major changes have already occurred in our expectations that have barely attracted attention. Some of us can remember the days when wives waited on husbands as well as children and infirm adults. Now, the days when men could not turn on the washing machine, boil water, or find anything, are gone – for the most part.

Able-bodied partners now take care of one another. Of course, if a partner is sick or disabled and needs special care, the healthier partner gives it or finds someone who can help. We seem to be all right with that change. We are now at the place where in many families women and men share in giving care to children and other dependents as well as sharing in paid work. This is happening even as societal and religious myths which support the traditional paradigm prevail in some parts of the population and in some parts of our psyches.

THE INFLUENCE OF THE MOTHER MYTHS

When caring for others was the primary work of women, women's work was idealized and put on a pedestal and then devalued in the realm of public policy and power. Motherhood was seen as God's gift to women and their being totally and lovingly absorbed in it was a cornerstone of family values.

When we begin to explore the possibility that the work of parenting belongs rightfully to fathers as well as mothers we are tampering with strong cultural, psychological, religious, and even biological world views that have had and in some ways still do have a powerful grip on our embedded thinking patterns.

Changes in behavior around the ordering of parenting work may, on its surface, look like just a practical and simple adjustment in family life. If along with our changing behavior we also begin to challenge centuries old perspectives, we can see that a whole paradigm is shifting. Only then are we likely to realize that we are engaged in a major social and religious revolution.

Facing those myths which have placed primary parenting responsibility wholly in women's hands is key to understanding modern parenting work. We need to address the myth of the Ideal Mother.

I have discovered an uneasiness in myself when tampering with the concept of Motherhood with a capital "M." After all, my own motherhood was and still is of fundamental importance in my life. Being a mother was central to my own Mother's being. Then I acknowledge that my father was of essential importance in my life just as being a father is vitally important to my husband. Still, I know in my heart that time has come for change, not in the critical place of parenthood in our lives, but in the ideal images that surround that parenting. The concept of Ideal Motherhood is not benign for women or men.

THE IDEAL MOTHER

We talk jokingly about "Motherhood and apple pie" as sacred givens in our society with which no one can argue – Motherhood being an ideal and cornerstone of both secular and religious culture.

But it is no joking matter. Living into the ideal of the Good Mother was seen as a holy calling. It was not only a woman's primary mission; it was a woman's definition. Somehow women knew what a universal Mother looked like, how she was to behave, what her responsibilities were, how she was supposed to feel and think, what her priorities were supposed to be. To know one mother was to know them all. Motherhood was written with a capital "M".

Of course no woman was able to live into the ideal no matter how hard she tried. But the ideal hung over women's heads as jury and judge of a successful life. Ideal Motherhood, it was assumed, allowed woman's true spirit to flourish, her inner beauty and strength to shine, and her sexuality to be contained. Women who challenged that ideal image barely made a dent in it.

The myth was a ticket for middle-class women's acceptance into mainstream society, which was their just reward for believing in ideal motherhood.

The ideal as it was etched into society's psyche goes something like this:

The ideal Mother is self-giving. She is selfless, finding her fulfillment in serving others. She loves with a sacrificial love. Caring for others is her life work. She is the center of the home and family. She desires nothing more than to make her family happy and the men in her family successful. When her children need her she is always there to wipe away tears, bandage hurt knees, hand out cookies or carrots, listen to stories, answer questions.

A mother sees to the physical well being of her children. She makes sure they wear warm clothes in winter, provides dry clothes when it is raining. She feeds her children well, paying attention to nutrition. She is the family shopper who makes sure her children have what they need.

She is responsible for her children's moral and spiritual development and their social adaptation. She fits her schedule around her children's activities and her worth is measured by their achievements.

At the same time that a mother is attentive and available, she needs to be very careful not to "swallow" her children. She cannot be overprotective. She must give them room to grow and never intrude on their space. She must recognize that being sheltered as she is, she cannot speak authoritatively about the "things of the world." That is not her realm. That is father's province. She is valued for her intuition, not her intelligence.

In short, mother is all-giving, all-present yet unobtrusive, modest, pure, faithful, unsullied by the world, strong in her moral bearing as far as private morals are concerned (public morals are beyond her experience). A good mother is protective of her domain, yet always in need of support and protection herself because she is economically dependent on her husband. Her social place in the world is determined by her husband's status. Being valued by her husband and loved by her children is her crowning glory. In an extensive pamphlet on the Ideal Christian Mother I picked up while waiting in a doctor's office years ago, I found the following quote:

> "God has placed an emotional capacity within a woman which is unknown in most men. A woman has a tenderness that works miracles. Perhaps a child has fallen and bruised his knee. Father tries to help with a touch here and a Band-Aid there, but Mother's simple smile of assurance accompanied by a little hug and kiss, works a miracle for the crying child.
>
> "A godly, loving mother is indeed a liberated woman; she is liberated from self-centeredness and lost in a ministry of love and compassion for her children and for others."

As a Mother, a woman is honored. Hers is the highest of callings. This far outweighs the fact that as a human being, she has been disenfranchised politically and economically.

In the preceding chapter of this book, we discussed the ideal image of the Good Provider. The Good Mother is the counterpart of the Good Provider. Together they have helped shape cultural roles and expectations for women and men. Because God is traditionally spoken of and imagined as male, women are elevated to semi-divine status as Mothers, following in the footsteps of all the women in religious traditions who have born male prophets and heroes, including Mary, the Mother of Jesus.

So goes the Good Mother myth. From a religious perspective, mainstream theology has exalted women as Mothers and ignored them as people.

EVE AND MARY

The idealization of motherhood served an important function in society. Women cared for children. However, it also helped cover-up the unconscious societal belief that women are, by nature, carnal and sinful. Over against the ideal of Motherhood is the concept of the feminine temptress, Eve. In Motherhood, the reproductive capacity of a woman's biological sexuality is celebrated and controlled by men in a patriarchal culture and her wanton sexuality is tamed, brought under control.

Traditional theology has seen Eve, created out of Adam's rib, as his downfall. She was the femme fatale who, egged on by the snake, led Adam astray in the Biblical story in Genesis. Seduced by the serpent, Eve defies God's will and in turn woos Adam away from God's will too.

Women as Eve's heirs have been defined as undisciplined, scattered, selfish, narcissistic, willful, unclean, and unbridled. Eve's sin, which ends human innocence, sets male and female against each other and relegates them to different work in different realms of being.

The sexual revolution of our time has done little to change this image. While it has seemed to take the stigma off of sexual activity, it has not freed women from being sexually objectified. Pornography, now easily available on the internet, continues to depict women as carnal and created to satisfy men's desires. It also depicts men as predators.

Mythically speaking, as a result of Eve's sin, women must submit to Adam and embrace their calling to motherhood. Redemption by Motherhood, either specific Motherhood or universal Motherhood, is women's saving grace.

Essentially, Woman is transformed, reclaimed, renamed, purified, first through being bridled in marriage and then through giving birth to children. Male children are her crowning achievement: Sarah, wife of Abraham, mother of Isaac; Rebecca, wife of Isaac, mother of Jacob and Esau; Hannah, wife of Elkanah, mother of Samuel; Elizabeth, wife of Zachariah, mother of John; Mary, betrothed to Joseph, mother of Jesus.

Jesus through his teachings centuries ago began to address these issues, enabling us to move toward a more liberating perspective on being a woman and mother. He did not see women as more sexually sinful than men. When a woman is accused of adultery and is about to be stoned, he stops the crowd from killing her by saying simply, "Let those without sin cast the first stone."

Jesus also made it clear that in God's eyes, women and men were to be held accountable, not for their biological acts but by their ethical being and doing. Women were not simply redeemed by motherhood.

"A woman in the crowd raised her voice and said to him, 'Blessed is the womb that bore you and the breasts that nursed you!' But he said, 'Blessed rather are those who hear the word of God and obey it.'" Luke 11:27 & 28

Jesus expects more of women than motherhood, though he honors caring for children. He expects women to be engaged in the fullness of doing God's will. Bearing children and nursing them is not all there is to being blessed. Jesus' views and the breadth of his mother's life are helpful in bringing an ethical challenge to patriarchal worldviews.

Eve and Mary each possess a different aspect of woman's sexuality which, when added to other aspects of women's humanity, are freeing and transformative. Adam, when he no longer has to live under the yoke of hard labor or rule over Eve, is free for his own transformation. Each is ready to be restored to being in the image of God. They are ready to hear God's word and keep it.

So, women and men, fathers and mothers, become the new Eve and Adam: We can see women and men as complex, whole people.

CHANGES OVER TIME IN THE MOTHER MYTHOLOGY

Shifts have been occurring in the ideal Mother paradigm over the centuries though its basic premises remain constant. Ideals and paradigms are never entirely static, variations keep them going and elusive. In the Christian tradition, Mary, the Mother of Jesus, has been seen as the prototypical dependent Ideal Mother, and, at the same time, the influential Mother of God.

Bishop Spong, in *Born of a Woman*, has this to say in its opening pages:

"Patriarchy and God have been so deeply and uncritically linked to gender by the all male church hierarchy that men have little understood how this alliance has been used to the detriment of all women. In a unique and intriguing sense, the parts of the Bible that have contributed most to this negativity have been the birth narratives of Matthew and Luke. These stories, far more than is generally realized, assisted in the development of the ecclesiastical stereotype of the ideal woman against which all come to be judged."

Bishop Spong sees part of the picture. There is another side, Mary as influential and moving women toward greater freedom.

In the story of the virgin birth, Joseph is a minor character. The real happening is between God and Mary and the child. Joseph is in the background and drops out of sight in the Gospels as the story of Jesus' life unfolds and Mother and Son become the embodiment of the holy family.

Mary is portrayed as a woman with power as Jesus' Mother. And, according to the story of Jesus' birth, since she conceives by Divine agency, she becomes God the Father's cohort. The absolute power of patriarchy is challenged and permutations are occurring.

In unmodified patriarchy, men controlled the home, women had the legal rights of children, men owned them both and could discipline both children and wife as they saw fit. In the case of a divorce, children belonged to the father. Over time, women have gained more power in the home as women have gained the status of legal adults, no longer their husband's property. But access to the public realm has come slowly.

Power in the home is important power but it is limited. Major aspects of society's decision making lie outside of the home. For women to have meaningful power, they need access to the public realm and respect as human beings, not just as mothers. And men need to take up a new and rightful place in the family. Men need a place at the table. Joseph needs to be reinstated in the family.

Amazing as it seems, it is less than a century since women obtained the right to vote. And as I write, women still cannot be clergy in the Roman Catholic Church, the Orthodox Church, Orthodox Judaism, or Traditional Islam. The ideal Mother image has not led to women's empowerment in society. The shadow side of "ideal motherhood" is female submission to and dependence on male authority, and political and economic disenfranchisement. Over time it all but banishes men as full partners in the home. And an issue that rarely surfaces is the polarization brought about by the chasm between the Ideal Mother and the Ideal Worker.

THE PROBLEM OF POLARIZATION INHERENT IN THE IDEAL

When families were large, and life-spans were short, it may have made some sense to divide family work so that women mothered and men earned money. (One could never argue that limiting women's rights was ever acceptable.)

However, in the section on paid work we discussed the problems inherent in dividing women and men's work into two spheres. The idealization of Motherhood required the separation of the domain of the home from economic and political life.

In the Introduction to *Loving and Working: Reweaving Women's Public and Private Lives,* Barciauskas and Hull say:

> "Women in our culture have been influenced by two conflicting ethics – an ethic of self-sacrificing love, deemed especially appropriate to women and family life, and the American ethic of individualism prominent in the male-oriented work world. Relegating the Jewish, Christian ideal of agape love to the traditionally feminine sphere of home and family has negatively affected our culture in several ways: (A) It has fostered an unhealthy neglect of self-development and care for the self on the part of women; (b) it has allowed

the individualistic ethic to reign supreme in the public realm, unmitigated by any altruistic concern for others and for the common good, (c) it has created an abyss for caring men and women between the other-centered ethic that they embrace in the private sphere, and the self enhancing ethic of the workplace; and (d) it has left women and men with no generally understood motivation for giving of themselves in the pursuit of beneficial social change".

Traditionally we have seen public ethics as having to do with justice and economics and self-realization, and private family ethics as having to do with personal morality, compassion and relational integrity.

In gender polarization, women and men were seen as "Separate but Equal," she with power in the home and he with power in the world. Women's realm and men's realm were not equal nor were the values they were supposed to embrace. Women's values were confined to the home along with women. In spite of all of our emotional investment in the "Ideal Mother," and our talk of "family values," we have not, as a society, often valued the work of parenting or the ethics we expect mothers to instill in children.

In order to be truly pro-family in the coming of age of our society, we really do need to demystify the image of the ideal mother along with the image of the ideal worker and reject the concept of separate and equal spheres of influence for men and women.

We can replace the stereotypical ideal mother with real parents caring for their children, living in the integrated worlds of the home and the public realm, balancing the best of the values culled from each.

In our evolving family system, everyone in the home is of equal importance. One-sided sacrificial love is being replaced with mutual love between adults. In this new ordering of life, society demonstrates how much it values the work of caring for a family by putting its policies where its rhetoric is and making it good and right for men to engage in this work along with women

A LOOK AT THE NATURE OF PARENTING WORK

Care-taking work is demanding and multifaceted, changing dramatically over time with the evolving life stages of a child and parents. It ranges from the very physical and constant work of caring for an infant or infirm adult to the emotionally, psychologically, spiritually challenging work of guiding young people as they mature. And ultimately, care-taking work can mean ministering to older adults as they face end-of-life issues often accompanied by physical or mental decline.

One new mother was surprised by the physical demands of her child in infancy. In *Mothers Who Work*, Jean Curtis describes that mother's experience.

> "When I went on maternity leave I had one of the people at the office bring work home for me during the six weeks. I had no idea that I wouldn't be able to get it all done. I couldn't imagine what a baby could do from 6:00 A.M. to 10:00 P.M.; what could take up that much time? I thought I'd probably have eight hours during the day to devote to other things. But I found out. One day at 3:00 P.M., I called a friend; I was still in my bathrobe and had not taken a shower or washed my hair or brushed my teeth."

As children mature, what they need shifts dramatically. There is an old saying, "When they are little, you have little problems; when they are big, big problems." Many parents of infants would disagree with this folk wisdom. But the parents of teen-agers might well see the truth of it.

Not only do children need to be nurtured in the home, they need to be prepared to find their place and moral footing in society. In an ideal world, all parents would feel equipped to ready their children for the world because they feel secure in society themselves and experience society as a secure place. But this is not always the case. Sometimes we find the world to be a welcoming place, at other times experience it as inhospitable or frightening. People along with their children inevitably face problems inherent in their context.

Areas where poverty is prevalent, or discrimination is a fact of life, or violence lurks around the corner, are difficult contexts in which to raise children. Parents in these contexts need special support and community advocacy.

Parenting involves not only contending with the external environment but drawing on inner resources as well. It entails trying to guide one's children at the same time that one is negotiating one's own complex transitions. This work takes place in the intimate setting of the home, in the midst of very daily and ongoing life, in the framework of intergenerational relationships.

Parenting sends us on an inner journey that cries out for self-knowledge. Parents grew up in families and were children themselves. On a conscious or unconscious level, having children of our own reminds us of our own experiences as children. Often those experiences tend to repeat themselves in our parenting patterns. The more aware we are of those patterns, the more prepared we are to live in the present, making decisions about how we want to raise our children. It is all right to see our growing up years with clarity and our parents with open eyes and hearts.

Family legacies contribute to our parenting styles and expectations. Part of this work has to do with making deliberate decisions about what practices learned from our parents to continue, which to leave behind, and what new perspectives to embrace.

Being aware of the models we have inherited enables us to be more intentional about our relationships to our children and perhaps more open and understanding with our own parents. Intergenerational ties are strong, and we can be more understanding and wise when we can imagine our own parents as children themselves. One of the most important gifts adult parents can give their adult children is the truth about their own lives.

We need emotional strength and relational intelligence far beyond what is required in the workforce to get us through this form of work. Family work is complex, as the needs of each family member intersect and sometimes compete, as personalities interact, and as closeness and distance are negotiated, as relationships change.

Parental work in addition to being so hands on and emotionally demanding is also administrative and managerial: coordinating schedules, planning meals, keeping budgets, paying bills, organizing family time and personal times, handling holidays, negotiating time with outside relatives, and overseeing those who provide for children outside of the home, to name a few. Add to the organizational work of parenting the need to decide how this work will intersect with paid work which provides for the financial support of the family, and with housework which provides for the physical environment in which the family lives.

Fortunately, caring for children is not work one has to or can do alone, even if one is home-schooling children. No parent can provide single-handedly for all of their children's needs or for the needs of other dependents in their care.

We all share family work with others – doctors, teachers, religious educators, camp counselors, baby sitters, other family members, neighbors. In its own way, family work is team work just as paid work is. Often, however, members of the team are quite spread out and the ones coordinating them all are parents. Parenting work is about preparing the next generation for life and it takes many hands and hearts to do this.

PREPARING CHILDREN FOR LIFE

Parents and all those with whom they interact in caring for their children are educating them for life and instilling values and ethics that prepare them for participation in society. Not only are we preparing our children to "fly" in the world, we are preparing the ground on which they will alight.

An important part of parenting involves engaging with society ourselves on behalf of our children, to shape the environment in which they will live out their lives: protecting the earth, promoting peace, advocating for human rights, supporting diversity, promoting religious freedom, participating in and valuing the democratic process. These and many other actions have to do with good parenting.

In the sixties, when the Civil Rights Movement was in full swing, the Rev. William Hervey went to Mississippi to help register black voters at a time when doing so posed a risk to his own life. The governing board of his church backed his going, but some in his congregation demurred. Bill was the father of seven children and they felt that he had no right, as a father, to put his own life in danger.

Bill said that he was going precisely because he loved and cared about his children and other children who deserved to live in a non-racist world. He cared deeply about the kind of society in which his children would grow up.

Bill and his wife, Beth, who supported and enabled his actions, were my heroes in the early years of my own ministry. Parenting inevitably spills over into the public realm and makes ethical demands of us as human beings.

Parents living in different situations and at different times make decisions that impinge not only on their family's immediate needs but on the quality of the world in which other children and their families will live. People parent by example and by acting out of their own integrity as well as by the words they say and the advice they give.

Parents who share in all forms of familial and public work or believe that this should be possible in the course of a lifetime are opening up options for their children. Their sons can be more caring and nurturing, their daughters can make contributions to society outside of the home. Creating richer relational possibilities in the family, and more diverse futures for our children, will have long term effects on society.

Many parents are sons and daughters who are already following in either their mother's or father's footsteps, mixing and matching qualities that they appreciate in all of the adults in their lives.

From patterns of co-dependency, family members are developing relationships of interdependence. Society still needs to catch up with these improvements.

Parents want their children to be happy and self-sufficient, to be fully developed as human beings with hearts to love. Shared work at home and in the marketplace sets a new paradigm for marriage that requires changes in the workplace. We open up new horizons for our children when we challenge the basic assumptions of patriarchy in the ways we live our lives.

Clearly, given the complexity and depth of parenting work, where possible, mothers and fathers need to do this work together. Fortunately, more men are engaging in active fatherhood and more mothers are establishing their own authentic ways of being mothers.

VALUING REAL MOTHERHOOD

In a world that can often seem so mechanical, so harsh, and sometimes so violent, real motherhood can seem like a saving grace. We all have a desire to be taken care of in the unconditional way expected of mothers. And most mothers care about their children's well being as much as and sometimes more than their own. The ideal begins to seem real until we acknowledge the fact that mothers are flesh and blood people. Mothers are women with identities outside of Motherhood. And yet motherhood makes powerful claims on women's lives. Giving birth to and nurturing children can be one of life's most fulfilling experiences, albeit with its challenges. Bringing new life that is wanted into the world can feel like a miracle.

I remember when our first child was born. I was so over whelmed by the wonder of this new life in my arms that I exclaimed to my husband, "I would rather be a mother than a minister any day!" I will never forget the day when parenthood was much more important to me than my career. Or the day when I was so impressed with what my body could participate in and bring forth!

I had the same experience again with the birth of our other two sons. I knew the power of motherhood from the first day of those births. I knew that, by the grace of God, these sons would be part of my life, central to my life always. I felt that nothing would ever diminish my need to be in touch with them and those they love as they grow up and become their own people. I wanted this to be true for their father too, something we could share.

I recall thinking then, and I marvel now, at how strange it was that after all those years of education and preparation for a career, I spent just nine months being pregnant and in that time one of the most wonderful things that had ever happened to me, happened.

How strange that such a common thing, an experience shared with so many other women, can be so uniquely important, so able to transcend so many differences, something we share. And how important it is to recognize that men's lives can also change dramatically with the birth of a child.

Here, it is important to note that not all motherhood or fatherhood is related to biology. Some parents adopt children, others are foster parents. Being a mother or father in love with their child does not depend on giving birth. Same biological parents cannot keep their pregnancy or child. As exciting as giving birth was for me, I discovered over time that the real part of parenting doesn't even kick in until a baby becomes a toddler, developing and growing over the months and years. And it is then that motherhood myths begin to take hold.

I am not sure when I realized that there is such a thing as "Ideal Motherhood." Motherhood is a powerful reality that does not need to be set on a pedestal and idolized in order to be a profound calling. Nor does it need to be separated from the profound calling to fatherhood.

As the raising of children proceeds, being a person as well as a mother or father reemerges, and if one chooses, so does employment, a career or a job. The all important work of parenting eventually needs to be woven into the whole fabric that makes up an individual's and a family's life.

Society as well as mothers and fathers needs to value the people who do this work as whole people at the same time that it encourages and facilitates care-taking work in families. Mothering is no less important today than it has been over the centuries. Today, we are becoming more aware of the value of the women who do it, the importance of the value of men's taking fatherhood seriously, and the need for children to be respected.

Parenting has always been a blessing and a challenge. Children are dependent for survival, have had to face, along with their parents, the personal, financial, and sometimes cultural difficulties they experienced. Some families have always struggled to make ends meet. Some families have faced discrimination of various kinds. Sometimes forces of nature intervened, sickness and even death, or violence in city streets or in military conflicts. It isn't just that mothers have not been "ideal," life has not always been ideal. And children are not all perfect. Even in situations that look great from the outside, inner struggles can be taking place and turmoil brewing.

Not all biological mothers or fathers are able to provide nurturing. Their own lives are too compromised and difficult. In those situations, others step in to raise children, with social support if necessary.

The mothers who do engage in this work can and do transform the images and expectations that are laid on them and in so doing actually benefit the whole of society. Some of the ideal notions have less than ideal consequences. I name just a few and leave the rest to be ferreted out by the reader.

Ideal mothers were called to be self-giving and sacrificial. One sided sacrifice is often a form of masochism. It is true that there isn't any form of love that does not ask us to sometimes set self aside for the well being of the other. Some self-giving is necessary for parenting. While we give to one another when we are adults in mutual service as equal partners in love, as we begin our relationships with our children, giving is unbalanced. However, over time, we try to teach our children to give back as they are able. That is a giant step toward their maturity and an important step in our own lives away from unilateral sacrificial love that deprives the other of reciprocity.

Too often, religious communities have encouraged mother sacrifice. Jesus' own life sacrifice was not meant to be repeated, but to end sacrifice. Loving others as we love ourselves is what is asked of us.

Ideal mothers were called to be compassionate, providing a listening ear, being a child's advocate, perpetually caring. Parents do indeed need to approach their work as care takers with great compassion. That does not imply a lack of discernment or doing for others what they can do for themselves or failing to hold them accountable for their actions.

My sister, who is a teacher, appreciates it when parents are concerned about their children's education and take an active and caring interest. She is dismayed when a parent is so wrapped up in their child that they are unable to see their weaknesses or misbehavior. At that point neither she nor the parent is able to be helpful to the child. Such indiscriminate advocacy is harmful to the child. Compassionate parenting does not need to be blind. Part of compassion is about discerning where truth lies and what our moral obligations to it are.

Ideal Mothers were expected to be healers. Parents are called upon to nurse sick children, to deal with emotional crises, and to be aware of their own behaviors that are in need of healing. The healing part of parenting was the hardest part for me. I nearly fell apart with worry when my children were sick or in trouble. Their father was much better about this than I was. Perhaps a good healer needs some distance. In fact, parenting requires both intimacy and distance, the ability to tell ourselves apart from our children. Ultimately, a healing heart and a critical mind combine to enable us to take life giving actions.

Healing also includes prevention. We are fortunate to be living in a time when we are increasingly aware of good nutrition, of the need for exercise, and the importance of personal hygiene. The invitation, "Eat, Eat," while well intended, may not always be the road to well-being.

The ideal Mother was very connected to her children. She was so connected that she too often felt merged with or lived vicariously through them. Eventually, mothers (and fathers) need to give their children room to find themselves, to be themselves, and to live apart from them. Being connected without holding on too tight, or letting go too soon, is hard. But that is another key challenge of parenting.

Mutual giving, discerning compassion, informed healing, and open-hearted and open-handed connection: not new ideals to live up to, just suggestions to keep us from falling head first into the "ideal" trap.

CLAIMING FATHERHOOD

Even though women give birth to children and nurse them, there is no reason to believe that they are the only ones fit for day-by-day parenting. Men qualify too.

In today's context, work is not neatly divided by gender. A variety of work patterns are emerging. Many men are developing deeper ties with their children than their fathers had with them as more women who are mothers are earning money. The arbitrary distinction between what it means to be a mother or father is blurring. We are side-stepping the Ideal Mother mythology.

Clearly, during the nursing stage of an infant's life, a mother can do something for a child a father cannot do. A father's bonding with an infant needs to be much more intentional than does a mother's in the early months of life. Though we have to acknowledge that even for nursing mothers, the learning curve can be steep.

When my friend's granddaughter was born, her son was prepared to participate in her care. He took fathering seriously and was looking forward to it. But in her first months, his daughter clearly preferred her mother's attention. He was hurt. Was it because she was nursing? Maybe the stereotypes were right after all. Biology is destiny. Hard as it was, he hung in, taking care of his daughter as she would let him and when the family schedule required. Eventually, as she grew older, his daughter began to enjoy being with him and wanted to be with him whenever she could. If he had given up when she was nursing, they would have fallen into traditional patterns and he would not have the experience of being as close to her as he is today.

In spite of the challenges men face in caring for an infant, many men have proven themselves able to do it. One man in our congregation takes care of three children, including an infant, on a full time basis. Another father shares care for two young children with his wife and a day care center as they both work in challenging jobs. In the movie *Jersey Girl*, a single father with a seven-year-old daughter struggles with career options and finally reaches the conclusion that parenting is the work he does best and enjoys most. And his gruff widowed father turns out to be a wonderfully nurturing man.

There is nothing in a man's hormonal make-up that disqualifies him for the work of nurturing children. Fatherhood, while it often includes contributing daily bread to the family, has evolved to include much broader and more fulfilling parenting responsibilities as motherhood has increasingly involved putting bread on the table too.

As children develop, men may be increasingly comfortable with their care. We have read that women are more relationally oriented than men. Women's culture as it has been handed down from generation to generation has indeed encouraged the development of connectional skills.

Carole Gilligan, writing about differences in men's and women's moral development in *A Different Voice*, has this to say:

> "Clearly, these differences (in women's and men's development) arise in a social context where factors of social status and power combine with reproductive biology to shape the experience of males and females and the relations between the sexes."

In our society, men may not be as culturally prepared as women when taking up the work of parenting. Nonetheless, they can hone their nascent relational skills. And not only do men develop parenting expertise, they also experience the same work-related frustrations that women do.

For instance, men caring for children as their primary form of work complain that it can feel isolating, lead to a loss of self-confidence, and be frustrating and boring in its repetitiveness and round-the-clock demands. Men like women speak of longing for adult company.

On the reward side, parenting brings with it the joy of interacting with children, sharing in the newness of their encounter with the world, recovering a sense of awe and creativity in life, and knowing the satisfaction of enabling and experiencing the wonder of growth and development of a human being. For those who are stay-at-home parents, there is the advantage of being one's own boss, making one's own schedule, and once the children are in school, using discretionary time as one chooses.

There is one big difference between men and women who parent full time. Women get more social support for this work than men do. After all, the ideal parent in our mythology is Mother. Women in our society earn approval for their parenting and are shored up in learning to care for children by the medical, educational, and religious establishments, and extended family networks. They are lauded for their achievements. There is no such clear-cut affirmation and support for men. We can right this imbalance.

A father, who had temporarily left work to care for their two children while his wife continued her research, told me about an experience that left him angry and frustrated. He was in a supermarket, shopping. It was cold in the building and he had a light blanket loosely draped over his infant daughter's face. A woman came up to him and lectured him about how he was wrong to treat his child that way. The stranger assumed that as a father he didn't know what he was doing. "That was not the first time it happened. It happens all the time," he said.

To call such fathers "Mr. Mom," is cute, but unfair. It assumes that "Mom" is normally the one whose job it is to care for children and it short-changes men. They are not doing "mom's work" when they parent, they are taking their own fatherhood seriously.

Many couples are living beyond stereotypically prescribed parenting roles and are doing it very well in spite of uneven support in society for their choices. Most fathers, like most mothers, are not stay-at-home parents. They are combining parenting with paid work. As more men are actively engaged in their children's lives, they are asking for family friendly workplaces that accommodate their fathering roles.

In *Working Fathers: New Strategies for Balancing Work and Family*, James A. Levine and Todd Pittinsky discuss the shifting values of employed fathers. They expect fathers to be increasingly involved in the care of children, to be the head of more single-parent homes, and to continue to take responsibility for infirm elderly adults. They consult with companies to make the workplace more father- and mother-friendly.

> "The father-friendly company is one that maintains a culture and programmatic mix that supports working fathers in both responsive and proactive ways. Father-friendly companies create climates where men and women realize that it is safe to bring up their needs to care for their families without being penalized. Even more, they foster an understanding that it makes good business sense to enable men to be good fathers, that work and family are not separate spheres for men or women, and that helping employees to be good parents helps them be better workers."

As we move into roles that seem right in the context of our particular family systems, we are expanding our concepts of "mothering" and "fathering" roles. As today's families establish their own working patterns, following their own hearts and reality, parenting is as important as ever, but the associations we have with the words "mother" and "father" are taking on new meaning. These words no longer carry the baggage of the past. Motherhood is a word used simply to describe a woman's relationship to her children; fatherhood describes a man's relationship to his children. Slowly, but surely, society is beginning to honor the parenting work of men alongside the parenting work of women.

Expanding the role of fathers in the home, and giving mothers more freedom to function in the public realm, can infuse both areas with more compassion and relational integrity, and a deeper concern for justice, efficiency and economic parity.

MOTHERS LETTING FATHERS IN ON PARENTING WORK: FATHERS TAKING RESPONSIBILITY

While mothers are parents who have identities apart from parenthood, the notion that they are the ones who have primary responsibility for the care of children can be hard to shake. As couples struggle to decide which of them is responsible for nurturing children and making decisions that affect their life, some mothers have trouble letting go of the idea that this is their area of expertise. Guilt accompanies any weakening of this concept.

The idea of sharing this work and seeing that men have some parenting potential or already honed skills does not always come naturally for some women. Sharing the care of children with husbands can be an exercise in trust that needs to be learned. Of course, there are those on the other end of the spectrum, women who, for whatever reason, are not able to take up mothering responsibilities.

The other side of the coin is that men have to claim their place as active fathers who are willing to handle not only day-by-day care, but also administrative duties. In a Working Paper from the Wellesley Center for Research on Women, Marshall and Barnett use the following categories as indicators of the division of labor for child care between parents: Overall Responsibility, Responsibility for Supervising Children,

Staying Home with a Sick Child, Arranging Child Care. Where both women and men work outside of the home, men who stay home with a sick child or arrange for child care are very likely to be actively engaged in parenting.

As couples raise children together, mothers and fathers need to have open discussions about parenting styles. Men may have more tolerance for physical experimentation than women do. But I have known men who are very protective. Sharing care also means sharing decisions and negotiating boundaries.

For years, the issue of whether or not children fared well in day care centers was up for debate. Many parents, and mothers especially, were conflicted about enrolling infants and young children in these programs or sharing their care with other relatives or friends.

Marshall and Barnett have this to say:

> "Research on the impact of child care on children has pointed to the importance of quality of care, rather than the type of care. The same may reasonably be expected to be true for parents."

Children do just fine in child care settings that offer quality care. Those in pre-school have been shown to get sick more often than the ones who stay at home. But once they are in school, the children who have been in day care get sick less often.

There is no reason for mothers or fathers to feel guilty for utilizing day care centers. What matters is that parents continue to see themselves as their children's primary care-takers and are actively involved with their children at the end of the day, on week-ends, and during vacations.

Jean Curtis, in *Working Mothers*, says that a mother's (or father's) working outside of the home for pay makes no difference in a child's development or happiness. It makes no difference in a child's attachment to parents. What really affects our quality of parenting is whether or not we ourselves are comfortable with working outside of the home.

Jessie Bernard comments as early as 1975, in *The Future of Motherhood*, on the problem of mothers who spend too much time with their children and the crippling effect it has on them, saying that such women tend to be poor parents and do not fare well themselves. They end up being frazzled, anxious, and depressed. Does that mean that all mothers should work outside of the home? Of course not. But neither, of course, should fathers. There is no one mold that fits all women and men.

AUGMENTING OUR PARENTING WORK

After a child's first five years of life, if not before, they are in school and the whole equation of family life changes. A parent's involvement in society can help a child find their own way at this stage of life. Joan, an accountant, said that her employment gave her children a sense of independence in that they were learning to take part in the life of the family, cooking and cleaning. She found that they were voicing opinions in family decision-making too. This independence led to more self-confidence in school.

Sooner or later, every family has to trust others with some aspect of their children's well being. All parents rely on outside providers to augment their care taking work: educators, medical professionals, entertainers, clergy, counselors, other family members, and friends.

Day Care Centers and after-school programs provide essential supplemental care for million of parents. After school programs support children and families during elementary school. By the time a teen is in High School, there are after school clubs, sports, employment, and, hopefully, a range of supplemental activities.

When I was in High School, an after school peace club, drama program, and sports activities kept me busy almost every day of the week, and they were all free. These after school activities are needed now more than ever, not by a select few, but by the majority of students.

I benefited from them even though as a family we did not need them. My mother was at home.

Those caring for ailing elderly relatives often utilize programs that provide care and stimulation for seniors during the day and turn to twenty-four hour care when that is required. Home health care of many kinds often supplements family care. Without this support, care-takers cannot maintain their own health and sanity and the ability to keep up with other jobs and family responsibilities.

As a pastor, I have often had to reassure parents and those caring for family members with chronic conditions that it is fine, necessary, and good for all involved to share care with outside providers. What matters most is the quality of care the people in their charge receive. For their part, primary caretakers are overseers who need to assess the quality of care family members are receiving. Making their concern clear, their presence known, and their expectations transparent, helps those to whom they entrust the care of those they love, to work cooperatively with them.

Life is so interdependent that there are many others with whom we share family care indirectly, and to whom we give little thought. We rely on those in the food chain who plant, harvest, process, manufacture, or market food before it reaches our grocery shelves. We rely on those who make clothing and retail it. Most of us rely on cities to pick up garbage and keep streets clear, and on police and fire fighters to keep us safe.

It would be wonderful if we could count on our employers to be part of our family support network by simply recognizing the care-taking responsibilities employees have.

Each year, the magazine *Working Mothers* gathers together a list of the 100 top companies that are family friendly. They have, among other assets, maternity-paternity leave, on-site child care, flexible hours, extended vacation time, reasonable sick-leave policies, and part-time jobs that pay medical benefits. These companies and others who are joining their ranks know that those raising future generations and providing care for those who are infirm deserve and need social support and are better employees when they get it.

Arnold Hyatt, when he was the chief executive officer for Stride-Rite, called such family-friendly policies to be in the "enlightened self interest" of corporations. Supporting workers as family members with responsibilities at home is good business. As a society, we need healthy discussions within families and in social networks on how best to support families for their care-taking work. These discussions can accompany conversations within families about how best to share care at home.

Rosemary Reuther speaks about the ways socialist societies address these issues and points out that:

> "Socialist societies have recognized that women cannot compete with men as equals as long as they are handicapped by the second shift of domestic work. They have tried to alleviate this handicap by socializing certain aspects of women's work. Most typically, this means state-supported day-care centers and nursery schools, which allow mothers to return to work within a year of childbearing. Maternity leave and guaranteed reentry jobs further compensate for women's work in reproduction. Some socialist societies have also experimented with collective laundries and kitchens. Low-cost or free contraceptives and abortions encourage family planning."

Reuther goes on to say that these government services do not insure women's equality. Women still work at lower levels than men, receive less pay and fewer benefits and do four hours more of household work in a day. One can deduce that in these societies home work and care-taking is assumed to be either women's work or the work of the state. It is not men's work. Until it is seen as men's work too there can be no equality for women and no real balance in men's lives.

Clearly our society, advanced in so many technological ways, will have to come up with its own solutions for supporting parents as they explore ways to share all forms of work. Providing political and community solutions is only a partial answer. Changing our attitudes and assumptions is another piece of the puzzle.

In a democratic society, we have a voice in elections and can use our vote to promote interest and concern for family friendly policies and programs. Where there is a communal will to accomplish something, we can find a way. The challenge is in finding the personal and corporate will.

Part of supporting the caretaking work of those who also work outside of the home lies in our expectations as consumers. It is not only employers who need to be sensitive to the family commitments of employees: consumers do too.

The other morning, when I got up I began to prepare for a nine o'clock dentist appointment. At eight o'clock, I got a call from the dentist's office, saying that the hygienist had a sick child at home and would not be in. At first, I was annoyed, it was inconvenient. Then I caught myself. This was not an emergency situation for me. We rescheduled for next week and I adjusted my attitude. Of course she had to be at home with her son, and what difference will a week really make to me? I have gained an hour of time today that I did not think I had.

A friend hired a contractor to do some work on his house. The contractor was in the process of renovation when he had to care for a sick child, delaying the work by a few days. My friend was annoyed just as I had been. The next day his son came down with a fever and it was his turn to stay home. He called in sick.

If we expect others to cut us some slack, we need to be prepared to do the same with others. Sometimes the adjustments we have to make are minor. At other times they are really inconvenient. Before we are in emergency situations we need to be aware of back-up services.

We all have to adjust our attitudes. Those providing services, producing goods, engaged in education, doing critical research, keeping government rolling, have lives and families and responsibilities that will from time to time require time away from work and inconvenience for some. We can expect this in our own lives and in the lives of others. Increasingly people are working in teams and can step in for one another as needed.

And here I want to add a special note. Supporting families sometimes means supporting parents who cannot cope with nurturing another life for a variety of reasons. Social support for them and their children can mean the difference between life and death. Sickness, poverty, and addictions take their toll on children and parents. Society needs to provide safety nets and we need to advocate for services for those children who are at special risk.

The fact is that all parents and children are vulnerable in one way or another at different times in their lives. We all need a compassionate network of care to support us at such times. Sometimes the extended family can provide that care. Sometimes that care comes from religious communities. At other times, it must come from a network of strangers, government providers, unemployment, fuel assistance, food stamps. Or special social services through organizations like Catholic Charities, the Salvation Army, the Red Cross. We all need to know, as caretakers, that when the need arises, there are those who can care for us.

THE AUTHORITY OF PARENTS

When parents share the care of their children with others they do not give up their authority for oversight of that care. Retaining that power is essential and needs to be protected because of the unique bond between parent and child. On one level this seems obvious, but it is an authority that cannot be taken for granted.

Jesse Bernard, writing in *The Future of Motherhood*, states that:

"One of the oldest battles in history has to do with the control of the child. And this 'battle for the babies' remains one of the most relentless in totalitarian societies. The Nazis fought a mortal combat with families for the control of children."

From an ethical perspective, parents have a fundamental right to oversee the care of their children. It is only when a child's life is in danger or severely compromised by their parent's behavior that the state has the right to intervene. From a theological perspective, children are a sacred trust, and the bonding between parents and children is a sacred trust. The home is the sanctuary of the whole family. In it everyone has a name. Everyone is involved in service to one another as each is able. There was a time when children were the property of parents. Today, parents do not own their children but they remain responsible for their care and have authority in their lives.

From a Scriptural standpoint, parents and children have a life long responsibility to honor one another. In the intimacy of family life, the fullness of a child's personality, ethical sensitivity and capacity for love can develop. It is also in this intimate setting that a child is most vulnerable and in need of protection. And as parents age, they may become vulnerable and need security and protection themselves.

Ivan B. Nagy and Barbara Krasner, writing in *Between Give and Take: a Clinical Guide to Contextual Therapy*, identify the critical importance of intergenerational relationships rooted in both being and doing. The authority parents have for the care of children is ontological, part of the natural order. It is critical that that bond be recognized and honored by society. Throughout life there are opportunities for transformation of the parent child bond through "discovering new options for relating, and making fresh inputs into stagnant relationships."

It must also be noted that the authority vested in parents is subject to law. Important and irreplaceable as parents are in their children's lives, their authority is not absolute. When parents harm their children in overt and obvious ways, they give up their authority and society becomes responsible for the protection of their children. That intervention must be carefully exercised. The state is an authority of last resort in the care of children.

THOSE THINGS THAT MATTER IN PARENTING

Sometimes when speaking about parenting we focus on irrelevant issues such as whether or not there is an adult at home full-time, whether a child is raised by a mother and father or a single parent, whether the parents are heterosexual or homosexual, whether parents are adoptive or biological. What is truly relevant is whether or not a child's interest and rights are being served, and whether parents are sufficiently able in their own persons to care for another even as they live their own lives.

For Every Child, published to celebrate the new millennium, depicts some rights of children, taken from *The United Nations Convention on the Rights of the Child*. In an introduction to the book, Archbishop Desmund Tutu points to the pictures that show children "happy, healthy, learning, holding securely to adults they can trust," and then to the pictures that depict children who are "hollow eyed, pot-bellied, as victims of malnutrition, famine, and disease; as bewildered refugees fleeing from the violations of their fundamental human rights," and goes on to say:

> "We are at the beginning of a new millennium. Let us commit ourselves to outlaw the conditions that have made the second kind of picture possible. The twentieth century has been known for its conflict, bloodshed, and strife. Let the twenty-first century be marked by peace and justice and development. Let us do everything in our power to promote the conditions that make the first kind of pictures, possible."

At the heart of parenting and care-taking issues are the rights of children. Parents around the world are called upon to be concerned not only for their own children but for children the world over. These children will inherit the world together.

In the list that follows, I have delineated some of the rights of children as set forth in the United Nations document and as we have come to know them through developmental theorists and social reformers. The list is in no way definitive. The full text of the United Nations Convention on the Rights of the Child can be found on-line.

1. A child needs food, shelter, clothing, and adequate health care.
2. A child needs a name and a place to call home.
3. A child has a right to education. Parents who share a child's care with other providers retain overall authority and responsibility for the care of a child unless by rigid legal standards they are deemed unfit.
4. A child needs to feel secure about their parents' or guardian's love. A child needs to know that they can trust them to be there for them over time. No outside force has the right to tear a family apart.
5. A child needs protection from anyone who would hurt them or be cruel to them, including mothers and fathers. And a child needs special protection in times of national conflict and war.
6. A child needs to be respected, to have a voice, to be listened to and heard, and a child needs to learn to respect others including the adults in her/his life.
7. A child needs to be able to live at his/her developmental stage, to be allowed to learn and play until they are grown up, and have their own responsibility.
8. A child has a right to grow up in an atmosphere that is reasonably calm and supportive,
9. A child has a right to worship in their own cultural context. And a child needs to learn how to make moral decisions and establish appropriate boundaries. A child has a right to ethical guidance that enables them to develop their own values.

10. A child who is disabled either in mind or body has a right to be given what they need to live happily in the world at their own level of competence.
11. A child has a right to rest, to create, to appreciate the earth, and to participate in community.

Along with these rights children need their parents to be as whole and mature as possible. They need them not only as caretakers but as role models. They need them to follow and show respect for just laws. Many different parental patterns can foster a child's growth and development as long as parents are committed to their children. Love is what matters most. And a parent's sense of well-being affects the well-being of their child. Over time, the relationship between parent and child can be reconfigured in the process of giving and taking.

Sometimes the work of parenting will seem overwhelming, whatever life-style one is living. These will be times when children or parents are sick, when vacation days are out of sync, when the demands of housework or paid work pile up, or volunteer work is crying to be done. But these times pass and parents learn to survive them.

Conditions of poverty, war, and discrimination make parenting extremely difficult. We are all called upon to end these states and to serve the needs of those families whose lives are caught up in them. Raising children draws on all of our human resources, personally and as a society.

As a society, we are coming to understand that what is good for the family is good for the whole country and vice-versa. Those in power are private citizens as well as public figures and have family responsibilities of their own. The division between home and public life, which has been clearly drawn for generations, is unhealthy for society. Public and familial moralities are coming together as we recognize mothers as whole people and men as active parents.

Without a doubt, nurturing children and caring for other family members can be one of life's most fulfilling experiences, one of its most daunting, and one that holds promise for the well being of society as a whole.

A FOOT NOTE ON GRAND-PARENTING

Love goes on and on. Adults with children are not only parents, they are also somebody's child, and potentially somebody's grandparent.

Generations are linked in complex networks of care. Parents continue to care about their children as adults. Adult children care about their parents. Where there are grandchildren, familial roles expand and a whole new dimension of family life opens up.

Generations can be a resource to one another in many ways. Grandparents can provide some perspective on the legacies they inherited and leave behind. Adult children and their children can engage with grandparents in shaping the world in which they live. Grandparents can be a listening ear for grandchildren and when it is necessary and fits, help care for them. Generations can provide emotional support for one another even across miles.

Parents as adult children or grandparents, while a resource to one another, can at times also be a source of emotional stress and discord. There are bound to be intergenerational differences and perspectives that require grace and wisdom to negotiate.

Over time, older generations may need special care themselves and adult children may be called upon to participate in making difficult decisions about the care of aging parents who will, hopefully, take some responsibility for thinking about their own retirement and aging.

When women did not work outside of the home, they were there for any and all forms of care giving needed in the family; children, grandchildren, siblings with chronic problems, parents. With both women and men working outside of the home, care-giving becomes a family matter and support from the wider community is essential.

Bruce Cohen and Michael Kegans, writing in *The Other Generation Gap: The Middle Aged and Their Aging Parents*, discuss the ways in which middle aged children care for their aging parents and give some helpful and insightful perspectives on aging. They point to the social systems in place to help with the support of physically or mentally challenged parents and the ways to preserve independence as long as possible.

End of life care requirements are not as predictable as beginning of life care requirements. In adulthood and aging, one never knows what lies ahead. Life is not predictable, we respond as situations require. Grandparents take care of grandchildren while their daughter focuses on her husband who is battling cancer. A sibling stays with her brother when he is dying. Another sibling assists his sister-in-law with medical decisions and provides a temporary home for her. A daughter helps her mother, in early stages of Alzheimer's, plan for the future. The stories go on and on and so does the work of care-taking in adult years.

I end this chapter where I began it. Family nurturance is a basic, essential, challenging and rewarding form of human work. We may love other kinds of work we do. This work is the kind of work we do out of love.

CHAPTER 6

VOLUNTEER WORK

The earth will thaw and flower
The rain will fall and feed
Dormant life will live again
In the season of the green.

VOLUNTEER WORK IS work done in service to the community, in the pursuit of an avocation, or in the pursuit of continuing education. It is unpaid, a fourth form of work standing alongside of housework, paid work, and caring for family members.

I have chosen to include volunteer work as one of the four forms of human work because it is labor that is essential to our well being as individuals and as members of a democratic society. Volunteer work is not play. It moves toward a goal, requires serious commitment of time, energy, talent, and sometimes money. People will engage in this form of work as they are able and motivated. For any individual, it is optional. However, it is essential for society.

In spite of or because of its voluntary nature, this form of work is extremely important and it would be a mistake to underestimate its value. Dr. James Luther Adams, ethicist and theologian, writes extensively about the voluntary sector in democracies. He notes that the "freedom of association," that is the freedom to form voluntary groups, is a cornerstone of democracy.

> "The Voluntary Association offers a structure for bringing a variety of perspectives into interplay. It offers the means of breaking through old social structures in order to meet new needs. It disperses power, in the sense that power is the capacity to participate in making social decisions. It is the training ground for skills that are required for viable social existence in a democracy. In short, the voluntary association is a means for the institutionalizing of gradual revolution."

Adams asserts that one of the first things a totalitarian regime does when it is taking power is reject this freedom.

For years, women were the backbone of volunteer work, doing it alongside of housework and parenting as part of their vocation. Men, spending their time as bread winners, engaged in volunteer work on a much more limited basis. Today, with as many women employed outside of the home as men, volunteerism now vies for attention with the other forms of work we do. The Ideal Volunteer as she once existed is no longer with us. Who was she?

THE MYTHIC VOLUNTEER

The Volunteer in traditional society was a woman. The Volunteer was usually married with children. Because she was not employed she could use her energy and talent to support local community organizations, especially when her children were in school. She was the right hand for clergy, she supported local schools, she started organizations to address needs in local communities, she joined garden clubs and gave leadership to women's organizations in religious communities and grass roots political endeavors.

She was able to organize people, plan events, teach, comfort the sick, raise money, sew for mission, and hold the heart of the world in her hand. She was service oriented. A woman, through the organizations to which she belonged, studied the world and became an advocate for the poor and oppressed at home and abroad. She often promoted peace and stood up for other people's human rights.

The Volunteer brought her "feminine" values and caretaking and homemaking skills to the work she did: making coffee, feeding people, caring for people, and organizing groups for education and action. The Volunteer belonged to networks of friends who met together to study, share stories, give one another support, and help others.

When women's and men's work was segregated and women were at home during the day, women were at the heart of the voluntary sector putting in the "man" hours that kept the wheels of unpaid community service turning.

Even though the mythic volunteer was a woman, men also belonged to voluntary fraternal orders which engaged in networking, community service and good works. Men made up the majority of members in the VFW, the Elks, Fraternal Order of Eagles, and the Knights of Columbus. They were in organizations such as the Lions Club, the Optimists Club, and the Rotary Club, to name just a few. They volunteered to coach and referee in volunteer sports clubs. Often, women belonged to the auxiliaries of men's organizations.

TODAY'S VOLUNTEER: CHANGE AND CONTINUITY

Society has come to depend on volunteer work that it cannot afford to lose. We can look back on the past and thank the women and men who through their volunteer labors did so much social good. Many of their activities have been institutionalized in religious and government programs and picked up by non-profit charitable organizations. We can also look ahead to ponder how the work they did will be carried on in today's world.

The Ideal Volunteer came into her own at a time when other doors were closed to her. She provided services and pursued ethical goals that were essential to improving our communal quality of life.

In the Presbyterian Church as in other religious organizations, women were excluded from holding official office until the middle of the Twentieth Century. They gathered in women's associations and made immense contributions to the educational and missional work of the church. While they could not be Deacons, Elders or Clergy, they exercised power through the work they did and the money they raised for the church as a whole. Women in all major religious organizations have provided a strong educational and charitable base for their organizations through volunteer labor.

Cheryl Giles in her book, *If it Wasn't for the Women*, has a chapter on the role of African American Women in the Sanctified Church. She says that their importance cannot be overstated.

> "The Sanctified Church rose in importance at precisely the same time that black women were organizing their racial uplift movement. In a sense, black women carried their Christian missionary zeal beyond the walls of their churches and into the streets and houses and schools of the community. For many women who wished to be missionaries in "Africa" – Mary McLeod Bethune to name one example – they discovered their very own Africans right next door. The uplift movement with its federations of women's clubs was the specialized political arm of black church women. During the period between 1896 and 1948, for black women at least, the church became a specialized religious institution while at the same time they organized a dizzying array of organizations that addressed every problem from scholarships and household domestics to the problems of international relations and the end of colonialism. The women organized homes for youths,

homes for unwed mothers, purchased club houses, and provided housing for women college students, established organizations of cultural refinement for household domestics, organized political clubs, campaigned for woman suffrage, and participated in a wide variety of activities designed to promote social change and advance the interests of 'the Race.'"

As the doors open for women to hold office in some of the courts of religious and political organizations, their role in voluntary organizations is shifting. Women's organizations still exist and are making significant contributions to religious organizations. However they are not as robust as they once were and some are beginning to reach out to men as partners in the work they do.

Now that the "halls of power" are opening up to women in most sectors of society, leadership patterns are changing, albeit at varying speeds.

Before Nancy Pelosi became a Congresswoman and subsequently Speaker of the House, she had a career as a stay-at-home mom. But that only tells part of the story. While she was raising her children, she was also engaged in volunteer work. Pelosi was born into a political family and was involved in many campaigns and community actions even when she was pushing a baby carriage. She now talks about using her "grandmother voice" in the House.

As equality for women settles in, volunteer work becomes the province of both women and men already stretched by engagement in other kinds of work. Time is at a premium. Given the importance of volunteer work, we are being challenged to think more creatively about how to incorporate this form of work into our lives.

Volunteers are still needed to tend the work of religious, educational, charitable, civic, and political communities. Volunteers are still needed to bring the arts and sports to people at local levels. Society needs the gifts and talents of volunteers. And many people need the outlets that voluntary associations provide.

One volunteer, Kim Whittaker, stepping up to the political plate, was a delegate to the Democratic Presidential convention in 2008. She says, "I realized how important it was for me to be with people who share my core beliefs and values . . . . the skills I have can really make a difference in politics."

Kim Whitaker continues the volunteer tradition. Like Kim, many of us are already involved and committed in the voluntary sector in some traditional and some innovative ways.

THE PLACE OF VOLUNTEER LABOR IN OUR LIVES

If we think of individuals living in a set of concentric circles, the family is at the center as our smallest and most intimate human network; neighborhoods, religious communities, social and political organizations at the community level form a second circle of networks; followed by institutional, national, and international networks; all surrounded by a rather amorphous circle of ideas, philosophies, myths, worldviews, and theologies that compete to hold the whole together and make sense of it.

Most of our volunteer efforts take place in the context of that circle that is community, that social milieu that serves to connect our families to one another and empowers them for participation in the wider world. Of course, this work can expand to engage the institutional, international, and theological level. It can be fulfilling, enriching, and empowering. Volunteer work is an avocation for many in which they can use talents, energies, and personality traits not utilized in other forms of work.

VOLUNTARY WORK AND EMPOWERMENT

Voluntary work allows us to have some power in communal political decision making. Through a variety of organizations we take up activities and causes that are important to us, affiliating with religious organizations, protecting the environment, supporting advances in medical research, forming community advocacy groups, extending our international connections, working for political candidates, and enabling a host of other efforts.

Through community organizations, people lay claim to having some authority over their living conditions and activities, and exercise leadership in ways often not available to them through their employment or parenting. Often we do volunteer work because we care about our children's future and believe that what we are doing will improve matters for future generations.

Community organizations enable volunteers to study issues, organize politically around them, and bring about change in their community. These organizations are the grass roots foundations of democracy. They empower people.

In his Doctoral dissertation, The Rev. Allen Fairfax makes a case for the importance of community organizations in a democracy. He illustrates ways in which they provide an opportunity for people to form a power base. From that base, they set goals and engage in dialogue with elected officials and affected institutions to achieve their ends. People gathered together for the purpose of improving their lives in community can be very successful.

Voluntary organizations have long served to work against all forms of discrimination and have empowered discriminated against minorities and women and those struggling for economic survival. At the same time, in our democratic society, voluntary groups can also form to protect their perceived vested interests. Groups can be at odds with each other's agendas.

In the 2008 elections for public office, it was heartening to see the number of people who engaged voluntarily in the political process, making phone calls, knocking on doors, organizing group meetings: everyone, of course, working to have their candidate elected and their perspectives and values represented in the halls of power.

The Internet has enhanced the work of the voluntary sector, connecting people in ways not possible before. The Internet offers new challenges, placing the burden of sorting out fact from fantasy or half truths on the shoulders of the reader. On the Internet, free speech and the freedom of association meet. Where its limitations and boundaries lie is currently being settled on a case-by-case basis.

We have power over what we choose to click on to, what we choose to post, how we choose to portray ourselves, and how we decide to network. Wherever possible, in the process of political empowerment, face-to-face meeting, when it accompanies internet connections, contributes to optimum effectiveness.

VOLUNTEER WORK AS ARTISTIC AVOCATION

Volunteer work can provide outlets for artistic expression through one's participation in musical, theatrical, literary, or dance groups, or through more solitary pursuits such as painting and sculpting. While artistic expression is employment for some, it is the source of a serious avocational creative outlet for others.

Providing a community with art is essential to its well being, enriching both artist and audience. In my own life, local community theater and access television has been important. In my husband's life, community theater and choral groups have been fulfilling.

Our son who is electronically gifted enjoyed donating time to video taping a local politician's conversations with his constituency. My cousin and brother-in-law are very talented wood workers. They treasure the time they have at the end of the day to retreat to their workshops. My brother-in-law has turned his wood working avocation into his retirement vocation. My sister is a quilt maker who finds time to teach others her art.

By day, one of my doctors practices medicine as his vocation. His avocation is playing in a jazz group. They cut CDs and play at community functions. One of my daughters-in-law who is employed as a biologist during the day, paints whenever she can find time.

Art is a form of self expression that enhances the whole community and enriches our environment. It can also be meaningful and empowering. Community Access Television is one example of how voluntary community art work can inform us and provide access to a powerful form of communication. Access trains the public in the use of media equipment, provides an outlet for their productions and prepares the public to view television with a critical and discerning eye. In a time when commercial television is controlled by a small cadre of people and organizations, local access provides a link with the local community and some alternate programming. While staff provide professional instruction and services at access facilities, volunteers do the bulk of the work and serve on Boards of Directors.

Volunteers keep community sports for children running as coaches and referees. Community sports play an important role in the physical and mental development of children and the adults who work with them. Sports also provide entertainment for parents and other family members who volunteer to support these activities. Some people see sports activities as a form of physical art.

Volunteer work is a source of community empowerment, enjoyment, and achievement in multiple ways.

VOLUNTEERS IN RELIGIOUS AND SPIRITUAL LIFE

Worshipping (or not) as we choose is a protected right in the United States. And religious organizations of all kinds rely on both professionals and volunteers for their survival.

I relied heavily on the volunteer contributions of both women and men as the Pastor of several Presbyterian churches. Every religious community depends on volunteers for many aspects of our congregational life, from worship to outreach. Through the years I saw a shift in the kind of work volunteers were doing. We had fewer bake sales, and annual fairs. We had more small-group meetings. And our service in the community was increasingly ecumenical as we addressed issues of common concern, such as peace, human rights, immigration, international connections, and diversity. But at no point could we have survived without volunteer leadership.

Most religious organizations meet weekly around the year relying on an ongoing commitment from members to be there on a regular basis. This offers an opportunity for families to gather in community with all of the benefits that confers, and, at the same time, it asks a lot from busy people whose lives are already demanding and complex.

When Friday, Saturday morning or Sunday morning roll around, people who have worked hard all week combining various forms of work can be torn between attending services and just kicking back or catching up with chores at home. Yet many choose to join communities of faith for the meaning they bring to their lives. Communities that could once take their congregations for granted now have to struggle with how to bring fulfillment to members and utilize their many talents without adding undue stress to their lives. The idea is for religious communities to provide contexts where stress can be relieved and released even as a prophetic and healing presence is provided in the wider community.

Religious communities provide an interesting case study of the evolution in the voluntary sector brought about by a revolution in our working lives. Religious communities are playing catch-up. We have seen an increased interest in spirituality in our society which seems to coincide with a decreased interest in mainstream organized religion. Some people want to be spiritual on their own without becoming part of a faith community. They can fit this into their own time frame with spirituality functioning in their lives much as TiVo functions on their TVs. And along with convenience, unattached spirituality permits people to form their own beliefs without needing to contend with the beliefs of anyone else. Too often, organized religion seems sterile and rigid.

This trend is being countered by those who value the importance of communal worship, children's and adults' religious education, support networks, and opportunities for putting faith into action. These are the volunteers who believe that in the long run, personal faith and communal faith are not meant to be divorced from each other and they are willing to try to hold them together.

At the same time that personal spirituality and individualized new-age pursuits have been growing, and perhaps as an answer to them, mega-churches have burst onto the scene. These churches have the financial resources to hire staff to do much of the work volunteers once did and to make sophisticated use of electronic media and marketing know-how. They appeal to our plugged-in and stressed-out society in special ways.

Still, moderately sized religious communities function in most communities. They do not have the finances to hire extended staff and exploit all of modern technology, but they are finding new models for fostering evocative and encouraging church life. Old patterns do not work anymore for volunteers. They are too time intensive. Most volunteers are not available during the day or on week-night evenings anymore. Of course, religious communities are grateful for those who are, but in order to reach a wide range of ages and employees, faith communities are changing, adapting to the changing working roles of women and men. By understanding the issues modern individuals and families face, religious communities can provide services that ease their way even as they utilize the talents people bring.

For instance, religious education teachers are working in teams, spelling each other so they can serve in shifts. Once weekly gatherings were the norm, but they are becoming bi-weekly or monthly. More meetings are being held after services on Sundays when people are already on site. More connections are being made by phone and e-mail and more "homework" is being done prior to gatherings so that precious time is not wasted. Opportunities for meditation, yoga, tai chi, and reflective Scriptural study are being offered.

Coffee hours often follow services so there is time for socializing and connection. Those who make coffee, both men and women, do it on a rotating schedule and more bought food is showing up at potlucks. And, depending on the make-up of a congregation, religious communities provide Day Care, job counseling and networking, tutoring services, after school activities and summer programs, and even minimal health care.

A local church has announced that during Lent, all committee work would be suspended. The congregation would take a sabbatical from obligations and if they desired, would gather instead in small groups where people could get to know one another and share faith stories, questions, and tradition.

Whatever our voluntary work in community is, we are learning to value people's time, make face-to-face connections count more, have fewer committee meetings, more opportunity for short term service, and make being together more fun and sometimes productive.

Some volunteer opportunities provide for solitary spiritual exploration while others serve to bring families together with other families, or couples with other couples, or singles with other singles or mixed groups. During the week, family members usually go their own way, coming together in the evenings for meals if they are fortunate. On week-ends they need opportunities to do things together and share some experiences.

Traditionally, men and women engaged in different voluntary activities and were able to make great contributions to religious life. What people seem to need most now are opportunities to engage in activities that support partnerships and families and speak to the special needs of working people. People need spaces and activities where they can get to know one another's families. Volunteer connections can enable this. In the context of religious community people can find opportunities for work that promotes and deepens their ethical concerns as individuals and as families for healing the world.

Education is another venue which provides for volunteer opportunities that enrich individuals, families, and communities. My parents were actively engaged in the PTA as a couple. Somehow that enhanced my connection to school and my education. And, there was something reassuring about seeing my parents working together around and caring about our education.

There are educational institutions that provide opportunities for adult learning that rely on volunteer teachers and organizers. I am one of the many volunteers who have taught in the Osher Adult Learning Program at Tufts University. This is one program among hundreds of others that thrives on volunteer work. Education is a lifelong endeavor and volunteerism in this sector is thriving, especially among older adults.

THE PUBLIC SERVICE SECTOR

Another aspect of Voluntary work takes place in the service sector where people connect their talents with those who can benefit from them. From reading for the blind to cleaning up the environment, people are serving one another carrying on a long tradition of service. Even though people from all walks of life and of all ages engage in this work, two segments of the population deserve special mention for taking on this volunteer work, young people and seniors.

While some retirees are choosing to be in the workforce in full time or part-time paid work, and many students have jobs along with educational commitments, retirees make up a large percentage of the voluntary service sector in the United States and young people are becoming involved in service projects at increasing rates.

The Boston Channel celebrating the voluntary contribution of retirees reported that retirees even live longer if they put in fifteen hours of volunteer work a week. The quality of people's lives improves as they reach out to others.

Another night on the news, college students joined by high schoolers were featured cleaning up a local river and speaking of how rewarded they felt by what they were accomplishing. Those who lived in the community abutting the river were grateful and pledged themselves to keeping the river clean.

I experienced student service projects first-hand when I was Chaplain at Tufts University. Students were engaged in a wide range of activities, tutoring children, putting on a community day, holding environmental activities, volunteering in soup kitchens, teaching English as a second language. They envisioned and administered these projects. Students at other universities are doing the same things.

At Harvard University, some students I knew were very involved in supporting janitors and service workers. Other students were helping out in a Drop-In Center, among other projects.

Retirees engage in many of the same service projects as students and also volunteer in hospitals and nursing homes, speak in schools about their professions, act as surrogate grand parents, drive people to doctor's appointments, and perform other personal services.

Sometimes young people and retirees have joined forces to multiply the effect of their work and enjoy one another's company. In the late sixties and early seventies, Maggie Kuhn organized the "Grey Panthers," an organization which brought elders and students together to engage in service projects and be a voice for those in need in the community.

For all who do this work, there is great satisfaction, and for those people and communities who are served, a much improved quality of life and renewed hope.

People volunteer time and talents in the areas where their passions lie. Major shifts in how the voluntary sector functions do not need to lead to a diminishment of voluntary work. Modern life styles along with technology that have brought significant change to our lives also open new doors of opportunity. Our connection to physical, geographic neighborhoods have changed at the same time that we are becoming part of new electronic communities.

CHANGING NEIGHBORHOODS

With both men and women at jobs during the day, our physical neighborhoods are sparsely populated during those hours.

When I was a child, I lived in a neighborhood in which we talked over back fences, hung out on one another's porches, exchanged recipes and news, and our parents looked out for one another's children.

When a neighbor whose yard bordered ours lost a son in World War II, it was as if we had all lost a family member. More than fifty years after his death, I discovered that members of our family, who put wreaths on my grandmother's grave every Christmas and Easter, still put a wreath on Jimmy Cursio's grave.

Before cars took over the roadways during the day, we city kids had a great time playing on the streets after school. In rural communities, kids played on the farm or walked in the woods. I have certain nostalgia for my unscheduled and free wheeling childhood but I know there is no going back.

It is not like that anymore. Children have play dates. Cars are everywhere. And safe places for children to hang out are hard to find. Some after-school programs provide opportunities for athletic and artistic pursuits but there are not enough of them to involve the majority of children. Malls and street corners are hang-out places for teen-agers.

Today, as an adult, I am sad to say that I live in a neighborhood in which I do not know most of my neighbors well. Most of us are not at home during the day to connect and look out for each other. While many of us have alternate communities, there could be value in reviving neighborhood networks.

In the summers when I retreat to a small town in Pennsylvania, I find that people still sit on porches, hold conversations across railings, and greet one another on the street. Most people are employed outside of the home, but there are more retired folk, more varied working hours, and a more relaxed life pace. And everyone's business is everyone else's business – for better and worse.

Even in small towns across the country, community empowerment through volunteer efforts could enhance life. And, in urban centers, through a little volunteer action, people could at least get to know each other's names. The better people know one another, the safer a neighborhood is, and the more alive it feels. Even where neighbors cannot be connected, voluntary organizations still connect us in religious, social, artistic, supportive networks at the local level. These volunteer communities are avenues through which we can explore our basic interests, values, and passions, giving meaning to our sometimes fragmented lives and reestablishing connection.

ENTER THE ELECTRONIC AGE

Enter the electronic age. At each level of human organization, our human connections are becoming less intimate, more electronic, and yet more diverse and frequent.

Walking down the street or taking public transportation, one is sure to find people on cell phones talking or texting. In modern American society, with internet and telecommunications of many types available in the majority of homes and communities, our human connections are both enhanced and diminished. Soldiers serving in Iraq can hold visual phone conversations with their families. Individuals can bond together in political campaigns or express political opinions on the internet. We can take courses, participate in book discussions, or "friend" one another on Facebook. We can play video games with strangers, do research, or bank on-line.

President Barack Obama, once a community organizer himself, understands the power of voluntary organization and took it to a new level through the use of the internet during his campaign.

What is missing through use of the internet is face-to-face connection. Voluntary work at the neighborhood and community level helps provide connections, essential to maintaining human relationships. And this work can be enhanced and extended by the use of electronic resources.

Aware of these changes, our challenge is to use new technology well in the voluntary sector at the same time that we encourage interpersonal connections. Of course, nothing can replace one-on-one relationships in the service area.

In our world when the majority of us are combining employment with family responsibilities, it would be easy for much face-to-face volunteer work to take a back seat. At times it can cause stress: the following story is an example of how stress in my own volunteer work found its way into my dreams!

In my dream, I was entertaining a group of friends. We were gathered for a purely voluntary church meeting, nothing to do with my job. We were enjoying one another's company and relaxing. As evening approached, I realized that I would have to scramble up a meal.

Meanwhile, in the other room, my son's friends were gathering to celebrate his birthday. I was supposed to join them. Mercifully I woke up as I was uneasily struggling with competing commitments.

A simple dream and very mundane. However, the conflict I felt was real and disturbing. I had to be there for my son and, at the same time, I had to make good on my volunteer leadership commitment. The stress involved was serious enough to show up in a dream. I understand the dilemmas in which we can find ourselves over competing claims on our lives.

Sometimes technology creates tension too. Time is time, a finite commodity that forces us to make choices about how to use it. I was meeting with a young couple contemplating marriage when the woman brought up the matter of her fiance's time on the internet. He was deeply involved in a community organization and was putting in many after-work hours on their behalf. She felt neglected. Balancing all forms of work with our important relationships and need for leisure and play is an ongoing challenge.

CONCLUSION

Women's and men's changing roles have had a tremendous impact on the Volunteer sector. This social change along with economic and technological changes is bringing about a need to rethink how we utilize and encourage the gifts of volunteers.

While one form of work, employment, pays us money, and two forms of work, housework and parenting, do not pay, we often pay to volunteer. Finding time to give of ourselves requires some doing. And as the economy tightens, our ability to give of our resources becomes more of a challenge. Yet these are the times when volunteer work in the public sector is most needed and appreciated. I am reminded of how grateful Jesus was for the widow's mite.

In spite of or because of its voluntary nature, this form of work is extremely important not only to society but to our own well-being. It can be fulfilling and integrating. It is connected with our democratic right of association which needs to be utilized and protected. It is also connected to our right to worship as we please and to gather in religious communities. Beyond that, volunteer work is connected with our human concerns for one another and our love and need for the arts.

Voluntary work in the non-profit sector provides some balance of power for institutions of commerce and government. People joined together can accomplish more than they can as individuals, though sometimes individuals can make a difference. People who form organizations can express opinions and work for change at an institutional level. Religious organizations, community groups, educational enterprises, artistic organizations, historical societies, all these and more bring a balance of interests and perspectives to our public life.

Work in the voluntary sector allows people to engage in public debate and dialogue over ethical issues: land use, public policies, methods of discourse, the directions of education, and other concerns as they emerge.

Our work in local voluntary associations provides a critical link between families and other networks, small and large. These associations provide grass-root human interaction and an opportunity for people's self-expression, religious expression, philanthropy, and empowerment. And perhaps most importantly, this work provides an outlet for the expression of our values and ethical concerns. We have the opportunity to create a society in which we serve one another and care about each other's well being.

A major concern of this book is the creation of a society that is more family-friendly, more protective of those combining parenting and paid work, and more accepting of diverse family styles. Much of the impetus for this change, can and will come from the voluntary sector.

We need volunteer activities in our lives more than ever, though many of our family patterns have shifted and we have less optional time. We will have to help the organizations with which we engage to continue to shift the way things are done to accommodate our new realities so we can be more effective. There simply are aspects of being human that can only find expression in the arenas of life that depend on the work of volunteers. Volunteer work keeps religious organizations going, democracy running, and artistic endeavors alive in our communities at the same time that it reaches out in service.

Volunteer work fills a need in our personal lives as well as in society. It enables us to participate in support groups, to find outlets for our creativity, to pursue our values and our passions, to practice compassion, to increase our knowledge and awareness, to gather information for decision making, to develop and use our leadership skills, to express and explore our spirituality.

CHAPTER 7

WEAVING IT ALL TOGETHER

It is all coming together now
The work of our hands and hearts
Joined seamlessly
Blessing and blessed.

W E HAVE EXPLORED all four forms of human work, the disappearing ideal images that have helped define them in the past, and the real people who bring themselves to doing this work in the present. We look toward a time when gender polarization will be a thing of the past. Women and men are fit for and capable of all forms of human labor. The challenge is to fit these forms of labor – housework, paid work, family caretaking, and volunteer work – seamlessly together.

In the traditional paradigm, simply described in the Genesis story of Adam and Eve, when we spoke about "work" we meant the varieties of work people (mostly men) do to earn a living. A woman's unpaid labor, housekeeping and parenting, was her vocation and a natural extension of her being a wife and mother. Now that Eve and Adam are come of age, they are each free to embrace any and all forms of work. They are free to see work, not as a curse, but as an opportunity, valuing all forms of work for the meaning they bring to our lives and the contributions they make to society. And neither Adam nor Eve has to rule over the other; they are free to be partners.

It is hard to overstate the magnitude of transformation involved in the movement away from organizing work roles by gender to organizing all work as belonging to all people. A gender paradigm that has existed for centuries, if not millennia, is being changed and challenged, almost overnight, as centuries go, though some subtle and some obvious shifts have been coming for a long time. The patriarchal ideal images governing the work women and men were once supposed to do have outlived their time. They can no longer serve as a blueprint for work in today's world. This is good news.

We are setting untapped resources free in ourselves and society, bringing greater balance to our lives, and exploring new dimensions of family love and societal compassion. Making choices about who engages in what labor in our particular family contexts takes more energy than falling into biologically assigned work roles.

On the surface it all seems simple. The majority of women are joining the paid workforce and men are doing more work in the home and taking parenting seriously. If this pattern holds, the change is deep and radical and new theologies and worldviews are taking shape. Our beliefs about human nature and our relationships with one another are being cast in a new light. And our understanding of Scripture and experience of God is entering a whole new era.

Religious communities that once saw traditional gender roles as God's will now have a moral responsibility to explore the theological and ethical implications of our changing realities as men and women who share in all of life's work. This exploration inevitably leads to a more complete understanding of what it means to move toward God's New Creation; what love is like in God's emerging Household.

We can eschew our belief in women's and men's "separate but equal" status. In God's Order dominant/submissive relationships are never acceptable. Love calls for reciprocity in relationships. That God who calls us to mutual respect for one another has respect for all of human kind and shows no partiality.

People in all walks of life, for a vast array of reasons, have been breaking out, and continue to break out, of stereotypical gender roles. Individuals are choosing work roles, and families are dividing the work of living, in a multiplicity of ways, sometimes making conscious decisions about who does what work in the family, sometimes adjusting work roles to fit external realities, most often combining desire with expediency. This multiplicity of life-styles, coupled with the integration of all forms of work, is becoming the foundation for a new social ordering of work.

How adults divide up labor and weave it all together in their family setting is not a moral issue as long as the choices made are mutually agreed upon and fair to each family member. (Of course, in emergency situations everyone does what they have to do.) What is a moral issue is justice in the family and in society. Society's facilitating the economic enfranchisement of all its members and supporting the nurturing responsibilities of all parents is a deeply ethical matter.

As individuals, when we move beyond the limitations of gender roles we have to cope with our own personal and relationship issues. Our moving beyond these roles brings about social change and significant alteration in institutional behavior. Anais Nin says it succinctly, "I believe the lasting revolution [in women's and men's lives] comes from deep changes within ourselves which influence our collective life."

As change comes, in addition to celebrating our expanding freedoms in our working lives, we may also need time to mourn. I have personally had to grieve the passing away of the old order. I could overlook the magnitude of change as long as it was just about my own life and life within my family. Now as I look around me, change is everywhere. The way my parents ordered their lives and the way their friends ordered their lives, if they could, is disappearing.

I know perfectly well that even for them and those before them, the ideal was just a suggestion and often an illusion, with a very dark side. But it gave everyone a model to aim for and a socially stable system to believe in. Sometimes gender polarization was the glue that held marriages together as partners fulfilled their duties to one another. Those who experienced traditional paradigms can feel nostalgic about "the good old days." They can, in honesty, also acknowledge the limitations of the way things were.

As we both grieve and rejoice in this time of transition, we need to know there is no returning to static gender work roles. We are moving on and this moving on is good for humanity and the planet. In the process, we are challenged to redefine and renew ethical boundaries, values, and faith positions to accompany us on this journey. A line by James Weldon Johnson, in the hymn "Lift Every Voice and Sing," says, "God who by your might led us into the light, keep us forever in the path, we pray. Lest our feet stray from the places, our God, where we met you; Lest, our hearts drunk with the wine of the world, we forget you . . ."

In the Mercy Center in Dallas, PA, where Sisters of Mercy live and work in a vibrant retirement and nursing community, there is a woven hanging commemorating a significant day in the lives of the whole community, the day the decision was made and finalized to sell the Generalate, their "Mother House," and move on. The hanging has these words on it:

> "This hanging was woven in 1979 by the participants in the Union's Tenth General Chapter during which the decision was made to sell the Generalate land and buildings. The vertical strands were originally attached to the loom constituting the weft. They symbolized the givens in our lives – the person, the times, our need for the shared word and bread, the call to justice. The weft threads were joined

in various ways by the warp threads which represent our decisions. Woven into the banner are grasses and twigs gathered from the Generalate grounds on the day of the decision. At the end of the chapter the hanging became a processional banner for the closing liturgy."

All of us enter adulthood with givens that we can think of as forming the weft threads of our lives. These givens can change over time, but they come to us as they are, ready for us to reshape. Then there are the warp threads of our lives representing the choices we make. These threads, the weft and warp, make up the tapestry of our lives. Life is a dynamic process and a kaleidoscopic journey. We carry with us the memory of old patterns and practices that we inherit, and process with them into all that lies ahead. In transition times, we need guidance for walking in the ways of life.

We, who are modern-day descendants of Adam and Eve of fabled religious fame, are opening a new social era in which we are free to explore becoming more complete, more fulfilled and more kind and considerate people. I can imagine the ancestors who have come before us and paved our way, cheering us on to choose life. New generations who are already embracing liberation are seeking to find their own way through the maze of ethical decisions they have before them. Nothing speaks more clearly about our commitment to future generations than our willingness to stand together with them in seeking justice in love and love in justice.

NEXT GENERATIONS

As adults live beyond gender roles they are educating children for their own adult place in life. We do not do this in a vacuum. We do this in a social context that may or may nor support our values. We can most effectively encourage boys and girls to break through gender stereotypes if we understand the power those stereotypes have wielded.

A few years back, I bought a toy stove and sink for my grandchildren, a girl and boy. I knew it would be fine for them to play with the toys together while they were small, and they enjoyed doing that. But when they were older, I knew it would not be socially acceptable for my grandson to play with the stove.

I remember how people looked askance at our son for crocheting when he was eight years old. My mother made some disparaging remark about it and he never picked up his crochet hook again.

We are all responsible, parents along with schools and religious communities, for the socialization of children that prepares them for adulthood. Even today, in the 21st century, it is still more acceptable for girls to embrace "male" activities and values than it is for boys to embrace "female" ones. Girls and women can change all they want but society will not change in critical ways until boys and men do. When both men and women change, power shifts, and along with it our attitudes and perspectives on power.

As children, we learn early what will be expected of us as adults. For our stereotypes to really change, the messages we give children need to be clear and unambivalent. But that is not always easy. Sometimes what parents want for their children must be tempered by what society will allow or encourage.

Before slavery was abolished in the United States, African American parents who wanted their children to learn to read had to forbid it. Reading could endanger their children's lives and tear families apart. In a heart wrenching scene in *Roots*, by Alex Haley, a black child who had been taught to read by a white child is discovered and forcibly, tearfully, torn away from her totally distraught and grief stricken parents.

Eventually, after the end of slavery, reformers and educators began to establish educational institutions that prepared young people for their full participation as citizens in society. Finally, reading and learning were acceptable for them. Some doors had opened.

In a different, more subtle way, sexism once kept girls from pursuing careers apart from marriage, motherhood, and service. Girls could be educated, but their rightful work was in the family.

If a mother wanted to teach a daughter independence, she would hesitate, believing the child's survival as an adult, if the family was not independently wealthy, depended on her marrying and pleasing a man. Marrying a man with good financial prospects was more than the road to survival in white America. Making a "good catch" brought a woman security and status. A woman with a career was expected to be single and celibate.

Parents had to acculturate boys by preparing them to earn money to support their future wives and children. Boys could curse and swear and act tough, within reason. They were being readied for a man's life in the economic jungle and political arena, and for military service in times of war.

The social messages given to children in order to teach them survival skills in society change from time to time and vary from sub-culture to sub-culture. In any society, parents can be out of touch with the world in which their children live, or in conflict with social norms. Parents can live on the margins of society themselves. And children, for a variety of reasons, can resist or have trouble with acculturation and maturation.

In *The Joy Luck Club*, Amy Tan explores the depth of intergenerational ties between Chinese women as they move from China to America and have to adjust to a new culture. She lays bare the tensions that develop as cultures and generations clash.

As we think about work and the shape of our working lives, we inevitably ask not only what work means to us, but what we are teaching our children about their futures.

We are blessed to be living in a time when gender stereotypes are breaking down. Today it is safe in the United States to imagine a world with our children, in which all forms of work can be shared between women and men – safe, but still not easy. We may have to search our own minds and hearts to know if we truly believe in this emerging new paradigm for both boys and girls. We know that employed mothers still don't have the social support they need, nor do parenting fathers.

In preparing our children for life, we want to pass on our deepest and most treasured values even in the midst of a societal climate that may be indifferent to them. We covet loving and secure relationships for our children. We want them to be able to utilize their gifts and live with integrity.

The physical responsibility of being a parent is challenging. So are the social, spiritual, and emotional challenges parents face as they prepare children to take their place as adults in society. We all raise children living between what society is and what we would like it to become. And our children live with what we would like society to be and how they see society taking shape.

The issue of acculturation is a tricky one. Most of us want to fit into the mainstream of life and obtain its rewards, and we want that for our children too. Yet we want to have integrity, and to stand up for what we believe is right. We cannot afford to be naïve. Breaking down some of the long-term psychological and emotional assumptions about gender and work will take time and commitment: the myths about Motherhood and The Good Worker, the stereotypical expectations of girls and boys that still exist, and the hard facts of the world of employment. Gender roles have been wired into society's generic brain; detaching them will take time.

We cannot totally erase the prejudice or any longing we may have for the remnants of the old patriarchal culture that still lie deep within our communal souls. We need to see the dangers of sexism as we have seen the dangers of racism and know that we must move on into a more egalitarian future for girls and boys that will enable them to be more whole people, to live more justly in relationships, and more responsibly as parents of next generations and citizens of the world.

At the same time that we reject rigid stereotypes from the past, we want to avoid imposing any one universal lifestyle on every family in the future. We want doors to be open. In their book, *Undoing Sex Stereotypes*, Marcia Guttentag and Helen Bray write: "Among researchers who study sex-role socialization there is little disagreement that arbitrary decisions about what sex role is appropriate tend to limit the development of any person to his or her fullest potential."

The changing workforce gives us an opportunity and a moral imperative, to prepare our children to live beyond gender stereotypes while we respect each one of them as an individual. We are also responsible for preparing our society to accept each person's full participation in society. As we do that, we want to be able to model new ways of approaching work in our own lives.

As we prepare children for life, and continue to make decisions about our own lives as adults, we know that life is not static. We live on a continuum of development and change. We can, even as we are living fully in the present, and making short-term decisions, remember to take a look at the long view.

WORKING OVER THE COURSE OF A LIFETIME

Over time, our working lives change as we change and as we experience shifts in the society around us. Sometimes our relational situations alter as well. Different ways of dividing up the work essential to family survival and well being will work best at different life stages and conditions. They will require revisiting with each change. A mother or father who may need or choose to focus on parenting work when the children are young may take up a career later in life. A couple who both do paid work and raise children simultaneously when the family is at home may change career patterns when they are older. A single parent may engage in all four forms of work for years and then remarry and change patterns. A married partner may suddenly need to cope with the demands of being a single parent. A person who never married may begin to do family care-taking when a parent or other relative becomes infirm. And, of course, our commitment to and time for volunteer work will vary over time.

When it comes to paid work, people will be invested in that work in varying degrees and that investment can change over time, sometimes by choice and sometimes by circumstance. Our working lives are fluid. We become parents and go through our children's life stages with them as we go through our own adult life stages. We all age. We plan as best we can for the future but there are situational surprises and sometimes we surprise ourselves. Health, the economic climate, current events, the weather, individual changes of heart, all are potential variables we face. Life happens.

In *Difficult Choices*, Carly Fiorina, who was CEO of Hewlett Packard and at the top of the corporate ladder, wrote about how her life was altered when she was fired from that post. She found new satisfactions in family life, especially as a grandmother. Her life patterns and preoccupations shifted, new aspects of life came into focus, and with them new aspects of her personality. They may well shift again for her, but if they do, she has reclaimed an important part of her life.

A cousin who became a single father with custody after a divorce, suddenly and unexpectedly became responsible for the financial, parenting, and housekeeping work of his family. I remember then-Senator Biden, speaking in the 2008 Vice-Presidential Debate, talking about how his life changed dramatically when he became a single father after a car accident took his wife's life.

When thinking about work, it helps to consider a life-span rather than a slice of life frozen in time. Sometimes life runs smoothly and sometimes it is full of surprises. Most adults, even if they take ten years to raise children, will have thirty years or more to work for pay or do volunteer work without primary parenting responsibility. Some adults will choose not to become parents. We have new options at every life stage.

Joyce Slayton Mitchell, writing about young girls and their career choices in *Be a Mother and More*, developed a pie chart suggesting the life cycle of their future. She begins with birth; continues with childhood and adolescence, both times for education; moves on to young adulthood, a time for career/marriage, and child bearing; all in the first 38 years. In the second half of life, she continues with career building and continuing education, until retirement. The circle completes itself with death.

This chart assumes that women will have children while in their twenties. It could be in their thirties or forties. The way the pie gets divided will vary considerably from person to person and family to family. And while her chart was originally designed for young women, it applies equally to young men as they think and plan ahead.

Throughout our lives, we stand a better chance of retaining the power to be agents within the limits of our circumstances if we keep the long view in mind when making even short term decisions. We can take responsibility for our attitudes and perspectives, our beliefs and values, our character, so that whatever choices we make, we will be as true to ourselves as possible. If we are in relationship, we honor and respect one another in our ever evolving process of decision making.

The essence of who we are and are becoming, combined with the times in which we live, contribute to what we choose to do with our lives and the legacy we leave for future generations.

FAMILY DECISIONS ABOUT WORK

Barbara Berg, writing on *The Crisis of the Working Mother*, (so often read when I took it out of the library that it was falling apart), said: "To be a working mother is deeply enriching, often perplexing and always pressing. It is a world intensely alive with possibility, exhilarating, beckoning. But for our guilt."

Men and women who live beyond fixed definitions of gender "rights and wrongs" as defined in traditional work paradigms and values, often have to face other people's prejudice and their own socialization and guilt. It may come as a surprise to learn that working fathers experience guilt even as working mothers do.

James Levine says in *Working Fathers*, "Whether in single- or dual-parent families, one of the common denominators among working fathers is feeling torn by two emotions: guilt for not spending more time with their children and worry about being able to make a living."

He goes on to quote a survey done by Jack Simonetti, professor of management at the University of Toledo who found that, "When men are unable to spend more time with their families, 78 percent of men say they feel guilty "often/always" or "sometimes," compared to 76 percent of women, who expressed more confidence in the time they spent with their children."

Balancing all forms of work in our lives is not always easy. Today, since families cannot assume that they will follow traditional gender roles, adults in families making decisions about balancing all forms of work in their household will face conflicted emotions. We have discussed each form of work as doable by either men or women. We have not yet spoken of what it takes to fit all of the pieces together.

For every family, the decision making process around issues of work will be different. The make-up of the family and its particular context is a defining factor. In some families, work patterns seem to fall easily into place, either by choice or dint of circumstance. For most families, however, the search for new working patterns will require some negotiation.

The first step in decision making is simply to be aware of what we ourselves want, need and expect for our working lives and our relationships. At the same time, if we have a partner, we have to be aware and conscious of what our partner wants, needs and expects.

I was in a group in which a man was asked, "How much housework do you do?" He answered, "As little as I can." A cute answer from some old-fashioned perspective, but I wondered what his wife was thinking or feeling and whether he cared. Had that arrangement come about by mutual agreement?

The next day, a male friend complained to a couple of us that his wife insisted on doing most of the parenting with their children. When he expressed a desire to share in this work, she simply said that it was her job. Clearly they would benefit from more discussion and discernment. She has not considered the fact that her husband might want to engage in parenting as his job too.

Awareness: it helps to look at ourselves and our situations with an honest and fresh eye time and time again. When we know what we need, want and expect as individuals, and have the courage to give voice to these things and the willingness to hear our partners out, making choices about work in a family context inevitably entails negotiating feelings and surfacing thought patterns.

I recall reading about a mother who found herself resenting the fact that she was doing all the housework while her husband read the paper. When she finally confronted him in anger, he replied, "Why didn't you ask?" Maybe she should not have had to ask. Maybe she could not expect him to read her mind. There are many "maybes." When the work of a household is being negotiated, there is nothing that can replace speaking our minds so we can come to some agreeable solution. Sometimes, even when we ask, we don't get the response we want or even need. The negotiating process takes time and a willingness to respect one another's needs and work toward fairness.

Our working lives don't run on automatic pilot anymore. This calls for increased face-to-face problem-solving and cooperation between all family members. In pre-marital counseling, I can try to tease out the expectations each person has of how their marital life is going to look, and what their expectations are about work. I can facilitate discussion and some give-and-take. I can inquire about support systems. But it isn't until time goes on, and the reality of family life sets in, that they discover in earnest what their expectations are and what resources they have to draw on. This is true even when they have lived together before marrying.

In my own life, I didn't really know what expectations I had about work until I was a few years and a couple of children into marriage. Nor was I aware of the extended family resources and church connections my husband and I could draw on for help. Furthermore, I could not predict the future and the opportunities and challenges it would pose. Throughout our lifetimes, we need to constantly revisit our agreed-upon arrangements regarding work.

Once we make decisions about work, we need support: family support, community support, workplace support. We do not have to live in a vacuum. Increasingly, couples and single parents are discovering the advantages of sharing work in the home and in the neighborhood.

Neighbors can exchange baby-sitting, handling emergencies, sharing material goods, looking out for one another's homes during vacations, car-pooling, even pet-sitting. I watch in admiration as I see my sister, her husband, and their adult children helping each other out in all of these ways. They are fortunate to be living near one another. It's all about working things out together as we can. We need to take stock of the resources available to us and find ways to utilize them.

When seeking to sort out work roles in the family, flexibility and adaptability are essential. Women and men being prepared for all forms of work makes this easier. Change happens, sometimes against our will. Then we have to adjust, sometimes to short term change: a child's sickness, our own illness, the weather, holidays. Sometimes change is longer: unemployment, chronic illness, divorce, ailing parents, natural disasters, job advancement, pregnancy.

In difficult economic times, we see an enormous increase in families needing basic material assistance. Asking for help may be difficult and require adjustments we are not prepared to make. The important thing to know is that when we get back on our feet we may be in a position to help someone else. Social support for families making complex choices about work and life-style as they face job losses, health crises and other unexpected changes, cannot be overvalued – whether that support is emotional, material, or spiritual.

Economic reality can be a deciding factor in some of the work choices we make. Whichever spouse has the highest earning potential or the most secure employment is the one most likely to be the family's primary bread winner. In a group discussing this matter, one woman said that her husband could make more than she could so she stayed home with their children during their pre-school years. Another woman said that she had done the same thing, but was glad that she had the tools to return to work when her husband lost his job. Another couple said they both wanted to be employed. A grandmother noted that her daughter was a high-earner and the breadwinner in their household and her son-in-law was a full-time dad. A single mother and a single father said that employment was not optional for them.

Everyone recognized that over time our economic situations and our employment options can change as can our financial needs.

One thing we can be sure about is the fact that there will be times in our lives when we face competing needs, runaway guilt, and resentment. Times when we turn off to one another. Times when we wear out. Times when we give up. These times pass. They are not usually an indication that we are tooling down the wrong track, married to the wrong person, hating our children, or engaged in the wrong work. These times simply are proof that we are human and need time to breathe and renew ourselves and our relationships. Though there are times when these stresses indicate a need for significant change.

In traditional families, traditional work roles often served to hold families together in mutual dependence. In egalitarian families, mutual commitment between partners is essential for sustaining relationship. Work roles can safely be negotiated or working realities accommodated when couples are prepared for the inevitable long-term changes in life and aware that unexpected ups and downs will come. We can also access society's responsibility and responsiveness to the reality of our changing life-patterns now and for the future. And we can work toward a more family friendly culture.

SOCIETY'S DECISIONS: FAMILY FRIENDLY WORK PLACES

Society, for its part, needs to adapt its institutions to accommodate this coming of age. We have already discussed some of the changes that are required as we move beyond stereotypes. Stevan and Ivonne Hobfoll have a good summary of family friendly policies in *Work Won't Love You Back*. They are not new. This was written in 1994; in 2009, with an economy in crisis and the future uncertain, it has become even more important to hold on to these practices. They are: Equivalent salaries for men/women, Opportunities for advances for women/men, Child-care (on-site, nearby, or a good referral system), Medical

Benefits, Elder Care, Maternity and Paternity Leave, Part-time/Job sharing programs, Flextime, Flexplace, Leaves of absence, Good sick leave policy/practice, Good relocation policies, Open phone policy, Employment possibility for both partners, Good vacation policy. I would add Transferable Pension and Educational Opportunities, Living Wages for full-time work, and Emergency Coverage.

As a society, we want to maintain safety nets for those who are unable to engage in paid work, whose full-time salaries are below the poverty line or who face unemployment.

We can give tax breaks or grants to companies that do job retraining, hire employees for their competence regardless of their gender, provide classes in English as a Second Language where needed, and in general, adopt family-friendly practices. Increasing numbers of companies are instituting such policies. Working Mother magazine publishes a list of these companies each year. They say that working fathers are asking for these policies along with mothers.

It is in the best interest of companies to adopt family-friendly policies because at least 75% of employees are in dual earner families. Labor Unions, for their part, can extend their interests and their advocacy to serve the changing needs of the American family. Voluntary associations that function in the public realm have a role to play too.

Religious communities are one of the few organizations in society that gather people of all ages together. They are in a unique position to minister to families who are making life style changes outside of traditional gender boxes.

If family is as important as generation after generation of politicians on both sides of the aisle claim, and religious leaders of all persuasions assert, then society needs to create a family-friendly social milieu. Life will get easier as we all insist on societal adaptations that fit our more balanced life styles and egalitarian relationships.

At the heart of all changes in both the marketplace and voluntary sector is a need for changes in worldview. We are on an evolutionary path. Theologically and philosophically the way we have viewed humanity and society is changing as we move toward parity between the sexes.

Inevitably, sooner or later, when we struggle with our choices related to work, we come face-to-face with the issue of how much money we need. How much does our family need to survive and how much do we need to thrive?

THE VALUE OF MONEY AND THE AMERICAN DREAM OF WEALTH

When my husband and I left seminary and he became the pastor of a small church, we had trouble making ends meet on his salary. In addition to our living expenses, we had educational loans to repay.

We discovered then that there is nothing spiritually enriching about living on the economic edge, especially when others are depending on you for life. We didn't have to choose between earning more money and having more time with the family. We needed the money!

I went to work part-time and the small salary I made did help to keep us afloat. Later, we shared equally in supporting the family. We moved from survival mode to comfort mode.

In his later professional career, my father was a lawyer for clients who lived on the other end of the economic spectrum. They had enough money to buy whatever they wanted including the services of a cook and chauffer. Witnessing their life-style up close, I saw that money did not bring them the happiness that I supposed it should. They were just normal people with more entitlements than most people have.

The lack of money is a problem. But having huge amounts of it is not the answer. There is a gaping disparity in our society between those with not enough money and those with money to burn. The middle class live in that wide expanse between poverty and wealth, with enough to survive and varying levels of discretionary money.

As Americans, we are fascinated by the rich and famous. Perhaps following their lives allows us to dream of someday being in their place. This is the Horatio Alger syndrome when anyone with enough initiative can reach for and attain stardom and wealth. But when we think seriously about our earning lives and what motivates us, striking it rich and being famous is a totally unrealistic dream for most of us.

I remember a conversation in rural Mexico years ago. As I was watching a missionary midwife deliver a child in a rural one-room home, a relative of the mother came over to me and expressed her desire to come to the States. She believed that everyone in this country was rich. And indeed, compared with those women in a home on an isolated mountain in Mexico, most of us are very well off materially.

But even in the States, our streets are not paved with gold and the majority of people who live here and those who immigrate are one (perhaps two) jobs away from poverty. There are many who are financially poor among us, including some who work full time.

We, like that woman in Mexico, have our own golden dreams, and sometimes imagine ourselves living in the lap of luxury. That dream loses sight of reality. Increasingly, we are being forced to face economic realities, face the destructive nature of exorbitant greed, uncontrolled consumerism, and examine our core values. We are beginning to make hard decisions about living beyond our means and trying to save for the future.

We can and do embrace dreams that are not based on the acquisition of material things, many of which cannot be achieved by paid work. We value love and time together in families. We can participate in causes we feel passionately about. We can embrace religious faith, we can form supportive communities. We can enjoy our children. We can protect Sabbath time and time for play. And we can find deep satisfaction in the work that we do if we follow our hearts and our talents. The list is endless. Money is not everything, though having enough to get by on is essential.

Increasingly, many middle class families are embracing a simpler life style than is encouraged by media hype in our plugged in, materialistic culture. Still, most of us who can afford to be, and even those who can't, are driven to want the latest in electronic equipment when it comes to cell phones, TVs, video games, computers, music. All of these can be costly. And we have been conditioned to accept obsolescence as inevitable.

Parents face a dilemma at gift-giving times when the cost of most everything their children want can be beyond their means. Maybe we could find really creative ways to share second-hand electronic goods when some of us up-grade, and move toward a time when obsolescence is not built into everything we own.

We are a society in desperate need of letting go of our obsession with the rich to make peace with enough, and be more grateful for who we are and what we have. Perhaps we can read about celebrities and watch shows about their lives as a harmless hobby: but at the same time, we can give the poor more respect and political attention, and give the middle class credit for being the real backbone of society.

While the number of people earning over a million dollars a year has risen dramatically in the last five years, so has the number of people struggling to survive, undergoing bankruptcy, and trying to manage large credit card and mortgage debt. Even those with a million dollars in assets are closer to the poor than they are to the 10% of Americans who control this nation's wealth. Billionaires are 1,000 times richer than millionaires, millionaires are only 20 times richer than those making $50,000, and those making $50,000 are 3 times richer than those making the minimum wage.

I suppose it stands to reason that the "middle class" would rather identify with the wealthy than the poor, but realistically speaking, it is delusional. An economic recession quickly teaches us that truth.

Any serious discussion of our working lives and the choices we make has to take into account our attitudes toward what is important in life. As we make decisions about our employment and opt as often as we can for that work which really brings us happiness, or time with the family, or opportunity for avocations, we are often accepting a more modest standard of living.

Speaking from a religious perspective, the linkage of money and power is an ethical one. It is not money that gets us in trouble but our love of money, according to Jesus.

Jesus didn't value people according to their social standing. People, including vulnerable children, were valuable in his eyes just because they existed. Wealth was not an essential human virtue or value. And those who had it, and were counted among his followers, were known for using their resources for the common good.

None of this suggests that it is wrong to want to be paid well for the work we do or to want the security that money can bring. Having financial stability and not having to worry day-by-day about survival is freeing and a condition we desire for everyone. The problems we have with money center around its place in our lives when we want more than we can even use. Then we have to ask about the lengths we are willing to go to obtain it, how much of it we are willing to share when we have it, and whether having wealth causes us to think more highly of ourselves than we ought and to act with impunity around issues of power. Money itself is not evil. Wanting to be adequately compensated for our employment is our human right. However, we can remember Jesus' point when he asked what it benefits anyone to gain the whole world and lose their soul.

When couples have the opportunity to break out of stereotypes and work as they choose within their particular context, valuing all forms of work including those that do not bring in an income, new priorities emerge and new possibilities begin to take shape. That will give them more options for a fulfilling life.

Increasingly, people are willing to trade money for time. And they are concerned not just with "bread and butter" issues in the marketplace, but with the issues of "bread and roses." Their quality of life matters and that quality goes far beyond material wealth.

As we wrestle with our working life choices we inevitably come face-to-face with the ways in which our private lives and our public lives are interconnected. Our quality of life is intrinsically connected with our ability to integrate our private and public selves and social systems.

INTEGRATING PUBLIC AND PRIVATE REALMS

The blending of the best of so-called male and female characteristics in our individual lives, as we participate in both the home and the public realm, is good for society. No human being is purely "masculine" or "feminine." We each have within us the capacity for true wholeness. Bringing this wholeness to our common life is a key to societal health.

In a traditional ordering of roles by gender, men and women were expected to carry out their social responsibilities with different sets of values. We developed and accepted a world in which different moral standards applied to the home and to the world.

The more sophisticated we became, the more serious the problem became. The world of industrial, technological, and electronic development became more mechanistic and impersonal as time went on. We developed ever more deadly weapons and more impersonal ways of delivering death. Society seemed therefore to be ever more dependent on what were seen as women's strengths in connection for the humanization of society.

This led to a subliminal fear that if women became more like men, we would lose our grasp on a compassionate society. We were also afraid of men becoming more like women. We did not want men to lose their edge, their power, their "masculinity." If we stop to think about it, women's values when restricted to the home cannot humanize the public sphere. And men's power, as long as it is the power to deliver death, is dangerous without the power to serve life-giving and life-enhancing ends. As long as men and women's influence exists in different spheres and we see women and men as imbued with different values, we live with values that are conflicted to the point of being meaningless – or harmful.

Now, if women do become more complete, and men more complete, we can explore having unified values and stop worrying.

Those who have wanted to keep "feminine values" out of public decision-making, calling them unrealistic and too ideal, and praised them only when they were held up as values in home and church were misguided. The values that are good for the home are good for the world, and rather than being too idealistic are pragmatically valuable, even essential. By the same token, some of the "masculine values" that have been upheld in the public arena and associated with "power over," can be used for "power with" to the benefit of both the home and public realm.

The peace one desires in the family can be a priority in the world. The cooperation that one hopes for in the family can be practiced between nations. The housekeeping that beautifies homes can be extended to help save the environment.

The ordering and efficiency of the business world can help address stress and chaos in the home. The teamwork that exists in the world of paid work can be a model for family work. The children who are so carefully nurtured and protected during their early years of life can be protected in late adolescence and through adulthood and not sent into harm's way.

The moral values of caring and nurturing that are cherished for the home can extend into public life. The moral value of extending one's self in a job, or maximizing production and creating material and societal well-being can serve family life.

The health of the family depends on the well being of every member in it and on the health of society as a whole. We are developing a concern for the natural environment and the sustainability of the planet that can be accompanied by a similar concern for our sustainability as people. The subordinate/dominant relationships which defined women's and men's connection in the past (along with their gender polarization) are not sustainable in the future.

Women and men are created for interdependence and not for mutual and exclusive dependency. Each woman or man is not created to be half a person until completed by the other sex. We are each meant to be whole human beings. We can enter into genuine "I-Thou" relationships and reciprocal intimacy when we develop our own autonomy and sense of self. That opens the door for our being true helpmates for one another. It also opens the door for the economic and parental enfranchisement of all.

If we can imagine a society in which men and women are encouraged to share all forms of work and hold life-sustaining values together, then we can create a society in which all those making public and economic decisions take family responsibilities into account. And all those who run families do so with the well-being of the wider world in mind.

When we covet the talents of every member of society for the good of all, no one's life can be circumscribed or disposable. When we see ourselves as servants of one another, we will not need a servant class to boost our egos and will be less inclined to long for power and stardom for its own sake.

It becomes ever clearer that gender polarization is not just a problem for a few feminists; it is the bane of both men's and women's lives and over time has become a threat to human survival. We need to liberate ourselves. In the long run, the presence of active fathers in the home and of employed mothers in the public sphere holds promise for the evolution of a new, more mature social order with life-sustaining ethical values.

WORK IN PERSPECTIVE: PRIORITIES

Life is a spiritual as well as a material journey. As critical as work is to us, our families, and society, it is finally a means to and end and not an end in itself. Life itself in all its multifaceted dimensions is what we are all about. We are the subject of our labors.

Who we are contributes to our working as much as our work contributes to who we are. What matters most in our lives and in the contributions we make to society is the work we do and how we do that work. Bonaro Overstreet, writing about what work might be, says:

"Any work that contributes to the health and comfort of man could carry its own dignity in a culture that related work to the dignity of man – not to the power of some men over others. There is no work so hard or grimy that it has not somewhere, by someone, been done in love and pride as part of the experience of belonging. There is no work that is not menial if it serves small ends and shuts a person away from his human fellows." (Written before inclusive language became normative.)

Overstreet connects work to human dignity, to human belonging, and to performance in love and pride. From a religious perspective, every human being comes into life deserving to be respected. Our highest calling in life may be the preservation or restoration of this human dignity in the course of a lifetime. It might be said that on a very deep level, that is what love of ourselves and human kind is about.

In our beings, we can lay claim to self-respect, and doing so, we can acknowledge our belonging in a society in which all are respected, beginning with relationships within our families and extending into the community and wider world. Taking this affirmation, this attitude, this perspective into our working lives with us, whether we are caring for others or plying a trade, enables us to work with the love and pride of which Overstreet speaks.

We work in the service of love and life. We work because we are human and need the fruits of our labor without which we cannot survive. In all of our working we remember that we are the ones doing the work. Work is not meant to dominate us.

In the last analysis, James Hillman says in *The Force of Character*, whatever we do throughout the stages of life, as we age, our character is refined over time and remains the essence of who we are.

"What could possibly last through the events of a long life, remaining constant from start to finish? Neither our minds nor our bodies stay the same; they cannot avoid change.

What does seem to hold true all along and to the end is
an enduring psychological component that marks you as
being different from all others; your individual character.
That same you."

We can be imbued with a passion for life that includes but is not
bounded by our work. And when we retire, or are unable to work for
whatever reason, we have value and can still find meaning.

Seeing life in its fullness and completeness, we find meaning in
relationship, in connection, in sexuality, in spirituality, in worship and
ritual, in nature, in art, in play, in all that life offers in addition to work.

My brother, after suffering a stroke that made it impossible for him
to do paid work, still found satisfaction in ordinary things: making
cookies for the church, repairing windows, installing a ceiling, planting
a garden. None of these activities could be designated as anything but
voluntary work. They fell somewhere between pleasurable pastimes
and community service. He and his wife did have to move from an area
where the cost of living was high to a small town where they could
live on his disability check, adjusting to economic reality.

When I was serving as the Pastor of Clarendon Hill Presbyterian
Church, I often called on older members who were home bound. It
was hard for me to imagine how they could be all right with their
lives as circumscribed as they were. Gingerly, I explored the issue of
what it was like to face such a life change. Each of them, in their own
way, assured me that life held meaning for them in spite of their lack
of mobility. One woman in particular, who lived in a small apartment,
and spent her days gazing out of a window, amazed me. "I am content,"
she said. And I could see that she was.

SABBATH

In the first story of creation in Genesis, God created for six days
and rested on the seventh. In the Ten Commandments we find the
admonition to "Honor the Sabbath day and keep it holy." I like to

think of Sabbath time as essential to our human well being. An early author obviously thought that even the Divine Being needed time off and away from work.

Honoring the Sabbath includes having a spiritual life and being able to worship. I also see play as a form of Sabbath. (My computer wants me to capitalize Sabbath. I want to speak of Sabbath without a capital "s".) It is not just a day of the week, it is those times in every day that we stop and enjoy life, take deep breaths, meditate, play games, take walks, gaze at the stars or see images in the clouds, pray.

We can only do our work well if we set aside time for recreation and just plain fun. We can't live well unless we play as well as work. I have images in my head of the Nova Scotia parents of parishioners coming home from a hard day's work in the fields and getting out the fiddles and singing and dancing. I have images of people coming home and zoning out in front of the TV, being entertained and turning off their work-a-day minds. I have images of walks down city streets and times alone sitting on park benches or in the pews of a church.

I am extolling the virtue of Sabbath and play. I am concluding with a celebration of the idea of just being. In my own life, work has played a very central role and is still important to me: raising children, keeping a home, employment as a clergy person, volunteering. I love it all. Sometimes I have and do allow work to define me. In the end, I know that we are more than the work we do. We have an inner core of reality that binds all of the activities of our lives together. We have soul.

We are indebted to Gibson Winter for the insight that we are moving into a historical era, in which the prevailing overarching paradigm can be "life as a work of art in process." Winter says:

> "In creation, the quality of human dwelling takes priority over every exercise of human control or collective interest. In this sense, the artistic paradigm affirms yet relativizes both mechanistic and organicist interpretations of the symbolization of power."

Winter's discussion is complex. Important for our discussion of work is his vision that our lives, our work, can be creatively lived out as art in process. We do not need to seek dominion over creation or one another. Our lives can be transformative as we contribute to making our human dwelling sacred space in which the powers of injustice have no place.

We can cherish the work that we all do and the many different ways work contributes to our well being in this world. This work is done by human beings who have great worth in and of themselves. As we bring the best of who we are, beings created in the image of God, to the work we do, we have the power to contribute to the well being of planet earth.

OUR SERPENTINE JOURNEYS TOWARD WHOLENESS

In the course of the process of living, we never walk a straight line. We stray, we excel, we plod. Our potential lies in our ability to be most fully and divinely human. We are not all dealt equivalent cards in life; in our humanity, we work with what we have been given. To the best of our ability we confront those givens to be all that we can become. For those of us struggling with poverty, with past traumas or current violence, with physical or mental challenges, the journey toward wholeness takes great courage and strength.

Some of us are given extraordinary talents or material advantages. For those with special gifts, the challenge is to use those gifts for the common good and to remain ethically and spiritually centered in our own being. Jesus said that from those to whom much has been given, much will be required.

For a rare few, there is a gift living in us that almost uses us as an instrument of its expression. My friend Lynda Elliott has the rare gift of music: but it is her being Lynda that matters most.

In preparation for writing "*Women and the New Creation*" years ago, I studied the work of Dr. Karen Horney, an eminent psychiatrist. Horney described psychic health as a state of inner freedom. She goes on to say that the qualities of health include the ability to assume responsibility, to know interdependence, to be able to express spontaneity of feeling, and finally, to be able to participate wholeheartedly in any work, relationship, or belief that one finds important. She understood that social expectations often cause people to reject parts of themselves and to overdevelop other parts for survival. She identifies one of life's challenges as our struggle to find ourselves in the midst of society's false "shoulds."

Our movement in life is toward ever greater freedom and maturity, responsibility and interdependence, none of which are ever absolute. Throughout life we struggle with the false ideal images of our time, some of which have been identified in these pages.

None of us is ever perfect and we do not inhabit a perfect world. From a religious position: we do our best, relying on grace, to move toward abundant life in our serpentine journey toward inner health. On our journey, forgiveness is both necessary and possible. As we forgive and are forgiven, we shake off that which keeps us from wholeness. In our work as in the completeness of being, we are called to contribute to the good. Being human, we sometimes fail. Grace picks us up.

Personally, I am glad there is forgiveness. I am sure that in the course of my lifetime, I have made some right and some wrong decisions when it came to balancing my commitment to my paid work and my family and practicing the integrity of self. We all fall short. All of us, when it comes time to look back on our lives, could identify things we would do differently if we could live life over. If we could live life over, we would just make different mistakes. We never get it all right.

Of course, being human means doing some things well, even extraordinarily well. We are entitled to celebrate our accomplishments and offer prayers of gratitude for the good with which we have been gifted and which we have used well.

Breaking down the walls of gender polarization in the world of work is a direction in which we are moving that can contribute to our health and well being as individuals and as a society. Opening the door to all people to pursue all forms of work is essential to our valuing every human life, promoting reciprocity in intimate relationships, and seeking justice, mercy, and peace in the wider world. Housework, paid work, nurturing work, voluntary work, all can be done by either men or women. Each kind of work carries with it unique satisfactions and challenges. What we each do with the opportunities we are given is up to us.

Raggedy Ann has been one of my heroes since childhood. I liked that she was floppy and had a twinkle in her shoe-button eyes. I liked that she was no fashion plate. Most of all I appreciated the fact that she was adventuresome and part of a very lively, diverse and interesting team of dolls. I liked her interactions with Raggedy Andy.

In one of her very first adventures in Mistress Marcella's house, Raggedy Ann and the other dolls, when the coast is clear, go in search of something delicious smelling in the pantry. When they get to the pantry the door is locked. Raggedy Ann falls and needs some stitches in her head. Once she has been fixed up and can give the matter clear thought, she says, "I think the door must be locked and to get in we must unlock it!"

Our lives are adventures, works of art in process. Sometimes we come across locked doors. We can remember Raggedy Ann's plight, get our heads set on straight, and then proclaim as she did: to get in we must unlock the door. And then we open it.

RELIGIOUS COMMENTARY AS END NOTE

In the Jewish, Christian and Muslim traditions, we come to know God as beyond all human projections and images. God is "Other" and yet in us and near to us in Divine love and human love – in all life giving connections. In the Buddhist tradition we come to see ourselves as part of a universal ocean of life that is both in space and time and beyond it.

In all traditions, every person is valued for themselves and for their connection to the whole of humanity. As a Christian, I see this in the context of my own tradition and in the teachings and life of Jesus as one who lived in history and who is with us now as the Christ and Holy Spirit: others will see personhood and relationship in their own context.

We cannot define the Holy, the Sacred. We can experience facets of the divine in humanity, in creation, and in God's self revelation. Doctrinally, religious institutions functioning in a patriarchal time have referred to their experience of God in male terms and attributed so called "masculine" attributes to God, sometimes with secondary "feminine" attributes that give us a glimpse of another side of Divinity.

As we move beyond patriarchal culture, we can say that God is female and male, mother and father, son and daughter, brother and sister, friend and lover. And these are all metaphors for One who, while dwelling among us, is ultimately beyond our knowing. The apostle Paul says that now we see through a glass darkly, but the time will come when we see face-to-face.

Humanity, being created in the image of God, is human and divine. Creation is good. That goodness exists, however, in the context of our world beset by the reality of suffering and evil. Hope lives in the promise that goodness will and can prevail and have the last word.

Jesus portrays the Order of God as an order of just love in which all of the old hierarchies are transformed and people minister to one another. Jesus as the New Adam and the New Eve calls humanity to the reshaping and restoring of creation as did the prophets who came before him and those who came after him.

In faith we move toward the time when we, male and female, will know that we are more alike than different, and be reconciled. We are made for right relationship with one another, with all of creation, and with the Holy. In each age and each time, human beings order society. Among other things, we order human work. We are coming out of a patriarchal age and we have the task of setting the foundations for a new order. We are well beyond an age of innocence. Eve and Adam are coming of age.

A new breath of freedom is in the air along with a renewed responsibility for right living. We live in a present that for all its imperfections and messiness is precious and full of promise. More than ever we need to be in partnership with the Divine Breath of Life. Each step we take, each moment that we live, matters.

Throughout the codified stories of faith we catch glimpses of Holiness that heals the world. As surely as society changes over time so does our ability to understand the Divine. In Scripture, there are strands of transcendence, times when authors, by their own account, step outside of the limitations of cultural history into glimpsing God's realm. And there are times when the message comes encased in a historic context meant for those living in the time in which it was written. It is for us to wrestle with what those texts mean for us in our time. There are also contemporary realities that were not conceivable when Scripture was written. For insight on these matters we seek new wisdom.

God meets us where we are and also leads us to where we have never been, except in the visions we see and the dreams we dream. In God's order there is neither male nor female. That is a vision we are invited to embrace, the details of which are left up to us to work out. When we pray, "Thy will be done on earth as it is in heaven," we are among other things praying for an end to sexism and gender polarization, Adam and Eve's age-old curse. Adam and Eve are becoming partners in life. Letty Russell, in the *Future of Partnership*, says that God sets the stage for this partnership by forming a life-giving partnership with humanity

This may all seem like religious gobbledy-gook. But these abstract concepts have concrete consequences. They provide us with a way to look at ourselves and one another as women and men outside of traditional stereotypes. My theological ruminations and the reader's own hold promise for bringing meaning to how we see ourselves and how we live out our lives.

In a new work paradigm, the objective is not to reverse traditional roles, nor to simply open the doors of power and commerce to women as an underclass or the doors of connection and communication to men as a dominant class (though these are valid pursuits). The core objective is the integration in every human life of the best of who women and men have been and can be. To this end, we prepare for all forms of work and engage in them as we are able. In so doing we foster more mature and full human development in each and all of us, and more loving relationships between us.

While discrimination based on gender is still a fact of life in society, a new way of being lies before us. As Raggedy Ann says, when the door is locked, open it. Now that the door is opening, there is, gratefully, no turning back, though the road ahead will not be even or straightforward.

I return to a question of my early adulthood, "How can a woman do paid work and raise a family?" and add to it, "How can a man raise a family and do paid work?" In the course of finding answers to these questions, I have stumbled across a new day dawning. Life styles that once seemed to be exceptions to the rule are now flowering, enabling us to be more of who we truly are meant to be. Society is coming of age in a new era.

REFERENCES

Introduction

Study on Employed Women, Harvard Divinity School, 1977, Unpublished

Alves, Rubem, "A Time of Disillusion and Therefore a Time of Hope," speech given at Triennial Meeting of United Presbyterian Women in Purdue, Indiana, 1970

Jones, Serene, *Feminist Theory and Christian Theology: Cartographies of Grace,* Minneapolis, Fortress Press, 2000

Tutu, Archbishop Desmond, *The Rainbow People of God: the Making of a Peaceful Revolution,* Doubleday, New York, 1944

Chapter 1: My Journey as Prelude

Task Force Reports on Women, General Assembly of the United Presbyterian Church, 1969-1972

deBeauvoir, Simone, *The Second Sex,* Bantam Books, New York, 1953

Friedan, Betty, *The Feminine Mystique,* Dell Publishing, New York, 1963

Morgan, Marabel, *The Total Woman*, Berkley Medallion books, New York, 1976

Women's Coalition for the Third Century, *Declaration of Interdependence*, 1976

Kepler, Patricia B. (lyrics), Kepler, Thomas B. and Ruffle, Douglas (music), *Eve and Adam and the Curse*, 1975

Interlude

Leaf, Munro, *The Story of Ferdinand*, Scholastic Book Services, New York, 1936

Heyward, Duboise, *The Country Bunny and the Little Gold Shoes*, Houghton Mifflin Co. Boston , first published in 1939

Chapter 2: Seeing Beyond Gender Polarization

Simon, Stephanie, "The Role of the Godly Woman," *Boston Sunday Globe*, p. A16, October 23, 2007

Morin, Richard, and Rosenfeld, Megan, "With More Equity, More Sweat," in *Washington Post* series on Gender Roles, March 22, 1998

Cannon, Katie Geneva, *Katie's Canon: Womanism and the Soul of the Black Community*. Continuum Publishing, New York, 1995,

Lerner, Gerda, *The Creation of Patriarchy*, Oxford University Press, New York, 1987

Heide, Wilma Scott, *Feminism for the Health of It*. Margaretdaughters, Buffalo, 1985

Brizendine, Louann, *The Female Brain*, Broadway Books, New York, 2007

Pinker, Susan, *The Sexual Paradox: Men, Women and the Real Gender Gap*, Scribner, New York, 2008, p.16

Rivers, Caryl, and Barnett, Rosalind C., "The Difference Myth," in *The Boston Globe*, October 28, 2007

Lee, Sang Hyun, "Pilgrimage and Home in the Wilderness of Marginality: Symbols and Context in Asian American Theology," in *The Princeton Seminary Bulletin*, Volume XVI, Number I, Princeton 1995.

Melano Couch, Beatriz, Presentation to the General Assembly of the United Presbyterian Church, 1970. (Referred to as one of the first Latin American Feminist Theologians in Berryman, Bernard, *Liberation Theology*, Temple University Press, Philadelphia, 1987.)

Jordan, Judith; Kaplan, Andrea; Miller, Jean Baker; Stover, Irene; Surrey, Jane, *Women's Growth in Connection: Writings from the Stone Center*, The Guilford Press, New York, 1991

Smith, Archie, *The Relational Self: Ethics and Therapy from a Black Church Perspective.* Nashville, Abingdon Press, 1982.

Nagy, Ivan; Krasner, Barbara; and Cotroneo, Margaret, Continuing Education Seminar at Harvard Divinity School, 1973

Miller, Jean Baker, *Toward a New Psychology of Women*, Beacon Press, Boston, 1976

Heide, *op cit.* p.16

Doyle, Patricia Martin, in Reuther, Rosemary Radford, *Religion and Sexism, Images of Women in the Jewish and Christian Tradition*, Simon and Schuster, New York 1974, p.15

Doehring, Carrie, The *Practice of Pastoral Care: A Post-Modern Approach*, Westminster-John Knox Press, Louisville, 2006

Barnett, Rosalind C., and Rivers, Caryl, *She Works, He Works: How Two-Income Families are Happier, Healthier, and Better-Off.* Harper-Collins, New York, 1996.

Chapter 3: Housework / Homemaking

Guttentag, Marcia, "The Stressfulness of Daily Social Roles for Women" in *The Mental Health of Women*, Goode, William J., Academic Press, 1973

Oakley, Ann, *The Sociology of Housework*, Pantheon 1974, New York, p. 149

Chethik, Neil, *VoiceMale: What Husbands Really Think About Their Marriages, Their Wives, Sex, Housework, and Commitment*, Simon and Schuster, New York, 2006, p.116

McGinley, Phyllis, "The Ballad of Befana,"from, *Jacob's Well*, The Orthodox Church in America, New York and New Jersey Diocese (On Line)

Kepler, Patricia. Study on Working Mothers, Harvard Divinity School (unpublished, 1977)

Norris, Kathleen, *The Cloister Walk*, Riverhead Books, New York. 1987

Rabuzzi, Kathryn Allen, *The Sacred and the Feminine: Toward a Theology of Housework*. Seabury, New York, 1982, pp. 64-65.

Kirk, Martha Ann, "The Divine House-Keeper," performed at a National Meeting of Presbyterian Women in 2004

Okin, Susan Moller, *Justice, Gender, and the Family*, Basic Books, a division of HarperCollins, New York, 1989

Chapter 4: Paid Work

Erikson, Erik H. *Childhood and Society*, W.W. Norton, New York, 1950

Wyszynski, Stefan Cardinal, *All You who Labor: Work and the Sanctification of Daily Life*, Sophia Institute Press, Manchester NH, 1995.

Faramelli, Norman, "The Context of Labor and Leisure: A Protestant Perspective," in *Labor and Leisure*, Massachusetts Council of Churches, Boston, 1994

Dittes, James E., *When Work Goes Sour: A Male Perspective*, Westminster, Philadelphia, 1987, p. 94-95

Pleck, Joseph H., and Levine, James, "Masculinity and Fatherhood: A Dialogue Between Jim Levine and Joseph Pleck," in *The Network News* of Sloan Work and Family Research Network, Boston College, Newton MA, Spring 2002

Fassel, Diane, *Working Ourselves to Death: The High Cost of Workaholism and the Rewards of Recovery*. HarperSanFrancisco, San Francisco, 1990. p.4.

Lorenz, Kate, *America's 25 Lowest Paying Jobs*, Career Builders.com (Internet) 2008

Stallard, Karen, Ehrenreich, Barbara, and Sklar, Holly, *Poverty in the American Dream: Women and Children First*, South End Press, Boston, 1983

Warren, Elizabeth, and Tyagi, Amelia Warren, *The Two Income Trap: Why Middle-Class Parents are Going Broke.* Basic Books (Perseus), New York, 2003, p. 180.

Ellen Goodman, "The New Equality – in Unemployment," *Boston Globe*, August 1, 2008

Wertheimer, Linda, "Tufts Offer of Loan Aid Steers Students to Non-Profits," Boston Globe, Oct. 9, 2007

Farrel, Warren, *The Myth of Male Power*, Simon and Schuster, New York, 1950, p.29

Terkel, Studs, *Working*, Avon, New York, 1972, p. xiii

Kaye, Les, *Zen at Work*, Crown Trade Paperbacks, New York 1996, p. 52

Hicks, Douglas, *Religion and the Workplace: Pluralism, Spirituality, Leadership*, Cambridge University Press, Cambridge, UK, 2003

Lifton, Robert Jay, *The Nazi Doctors*, Basic Books, New York, 1986

Bianchi, Eugene C., article in *Journal of Current Social Issues*, November 1977

Ahmed, Leila, *Women and Gender in Islam: Historical Roots of a Modern Debate*, Yale University Press, New Haven, 1992

Chapter 5: Parenting

Spong, John A., *Born of a Woman: a Bishop Rethinks the Birth of Jesus,* HarperCollins, New York, 1992, p. 13

Barciauskas, Rosemary Curran, and Hull, Debra Beery, *Loving and Working: Reweaving Women's Public and Private Lives*, Meyer-Stone Books, Bloomington, Indiana, 1989, p. 4

Bodin, Jeanne, and Mitelman, Bonnie, *Mothers Who Work: Strategies for Coping,* Ballantine Books, New York 1983

Gilligan, Carol, *In a Different Voice: Psychological Theory and Women's Development*, Cambridge, Harvard University Press, 1982. p.25

Levine, James A. and Pittinsky, Todd, *Working Fathers: New Strategies for Balancing Work and Family*, Addison-Wesley, Reading, MA 1997. p.62

Marshall, Nancy L., and Barnett, Rosalind C., *Child Care, Division of Labor, and Parental Emotional Well-Being Among Two-Earner Families*, Working Paper 252, Wellesley Center for Research on Women, 1992

Curtis, Jean, *Working Mothers*, Doubleday, New York, 1978, p. 57

Bernard, Jessie, *The Future of Motherhood*, Penguin Books, NY 1974

Reuther, Rosemary Radford, *Sexism and God-Talk: Toward a Feminist Theology.* Beacon Press, Boston, 1983

Bernard, *ibid*, p. 277

Boszormenyi-Nagy, Ivan and Krasner, Barbara, *Between Give and Take: A Clinical Guide to Contextual Therapy*, Brunner/Mazel, New York, 1986

UNICEF, *For Every Child: The UN Convention on the Rights of the Child in word and picture*, Phyllis Fogelman Books, New York, 2000. Also see United Nations, *Convention on the Rights of the Child*, 1991.

Cohen, Bruce, and Kegans, Michael, *The Other Generation Gap: The Middle Aged and Their Aging Parents*, Fottett Publishing, Chicago, 1978

Chapter 6: Volunteer Work

Adams, James Luther, "Religious Man and Politics," in *Colloquy*, April, 1968

Giles, Cheryl, *If it Wasn't for the Women*, Orbis Books, Maryknoll, NY 2001, p. 85-86

Goodman, Ellen, "Nancy Pelosi's Powerful First Act," *Boston Globe*, Jan.5, 2007

Whitaker, Kim, "On Being a Volunteer," *Boston Globe*, August 28, 2008

Fairfax, Allen, *Challenging the Rules and the Construction of Public Space: a Case Study of the Merrimack Valley Project* (Doctoral Dissertation), Boston College, 2006

Kuhn, Maggie, *Maggie Kuhn on Aging: A Dialogue*, Hussell, Dieter, Westminster, Philadelphia, 1977

Chapter 7: Weaving it All Together

Nin, Anais, *In Favor of the Sensitive Man and Other Essays*, Harcourt Brace Jovanovich, New York, 1966 p. 28

Haley, Alex, *Roots*: The Saga of an American Family, (Thirtieth Anniversary Edition.)Vanguard Press, New York, 2007

Tan, Amy, *The Joy Luck Club*, Penguin books, New York, 1989

Guttentag, Marcia, and Bray, Helen, *Undoing Sex Stereotypes: for Research and Educators,* McGraw Hill, New York 1976, p. 11

Berg, Barbara J., *The Crisis of the Working Mother: Resolving the Conflict Between Family and Work,* Summit Books, New York, 1986

Levine and Pittinski, *op. cit.*, p. 21-22

Fiorina, Carly, *Difficult Choices*, Penguin Audio Books, New York 2006

Mitchell, Joyce Slayton, *Be a Mother and More, Career and Life Planning for Young Women*, Bantam Books, New York, 1980

Hobfoll, Stevan E. and Ivonne H., *Work Won't Love You Back: The Dual Career Couple's Survival Guide*, W. H. Freeman Press, New York, 1994. p. 259

Overstreet, Bonaro, *How to Think about Ourselves*, New York, Harper and Brothers, 1948

Hillman, James, *The Force of Character and the Lasting of Life*, Random House, New York, 1999

Winter, Gibson, *Liberating Creation*, Crossroad, New York, 1981

Kepler, Patricia Budd, "Karen Horney and Human Growth," in Kepler, Patricia Budd, and Schaef, Ann Wilson, *Women and the New Creation*, Concern Magazine, United Presbyterian Women, 1972

Gruelle, Johnny, *Raggedy Ann Stories*, Simon Schuster for Young Readers, New York, Reprinted in 1993

Russell, Letty M., *The Future of Partnership*, Westminster Press, Philadelphia, 1979

Breinigsville, PA USA
01 November 2009
226864BV00001B/4/P